MATHEMATICS AND THE PRIMARY SCHOOL CURRICULUM

Ernest Choat

NFER Publishing Company

Published by the NFER Publishing Company Ltd.,
Darville House, 2 Oxford Road East,
Windsor, Berks. SL4 1DF
Registered Office: The Mere, Upton Park, Slough, Berks. SL1 2DQ
First published 1980
© Ernest Choat 1980
ISBN 0 85633 206 2

Typeset by Datchet Printing Services, Station Approach, Datchet, Slough, Berks.
Printed in Great Britain by
Staples Printers Ltd., Love Lane, Rochester
Kent ME1 1TP

6·75

Contents

Acknowledgements		6
Introduction		7
Chapter 1	The Influence of Mathematics on the Primary School Curriculum	14
Chapter 2	Disagreements on the Teaching of Mathematics in the Primary School	26
Chapter 3	Understanding in Mathematics	36
Chapter 4	Interlude with Jane	47
Chapter 5	The Role, Responsibilities and Expectations of Teachers	50
Chapter 6	Changes in the Primary School: Their Effect on the Curriculum, and the Teaching of Mathematics	73
Chapter 7	Evaluation and Assessment	98
Chapter 8	The Expanding Landscape	122
	Index	126

Acknowledgements

I wish to thank those people who have helped towards the completion of this book. Although she is too young to appreciate her contribution, I am indebted to Jane for the glimpses of her mathematical development. My gratitude is extended to Mrs C. O'Connor and Mrs Gay Whent for allowing the publication of their versions of a teacher's role, Ron Waggitt and Carrol Hurdle for their comments and observations on the script, and Leslie A. Smith for his support of my work.

Introduction

Teaching primary mathematics is more difficult than
many outside primary schools imagine.

This statement, contained in an article (Choat 1977) for the
magazine, 'Ideas', was taken up by the editor, Leslie A. Smith, who
commented, 'It is about time somebody said this loudly'.
The article attempted to clarify misunderstandings about
mathematics teaching in the primary school, and spelt out the
challenge facing teachers. Nevertheless, although the editor's
remarks were complementary, they caused some uneasiness. It was
all very well warning teachers of what they may expect, but were they
equipped to meet the challenge? Teaching mathematics in the
primary school is not only a matter of mathematical content, but the
recognition of children as individuals, and an awareness of what the
primary school curriculum is attempting to achieve. Numerous
books have been published on primary mathematics but they have
concentrated on mathematics and theories of mathematical
development, with an emphasis on the work of Piaget. Likewise,
many books on curriculum theory have appeared, but mainly on
secondary schools and beyond. Mathematics and its influence on the
primary school curriculum has received little consideration. Too
often mathematics is treated as if it does not belong to the lives of
children. It is looked upon as a subject in isolation from the
remainder of curriculum content.
The mathematical revolution of the late 1950s and early 1960s
emphasized the need for children to understand the mathematics
that they were learning. In principle, this intention cannot be faulted.
If we wish to promote a competent mathematical society, we must
encourage the acquisition of mathematics from the earliest moment.
The young child is surrounded by mathematics. Mathematics is

everywhere and in almost everything, and he is dependent on
mathematics for coming to terms with the world in which he lives.
This emphasis is apparent in Nursery Schools where practically every
activity has a mathematical bias. In effect, more mathematics is
taught in Nursery School than in any other educational
establishment. The priority continues in Infants' School reception
classes with activity and motion that rely on mathematics but, later,
when learning becomes formal so mathematics begins to become
formal. It is at this stage that cracks begin to appear in primary
mathematics teaching.

Those people who criticize the education of children in primary
school immediately blame the teachers. They allege that many
primary school teachers do not have the necessary mathematical
background to give justice to the subject, and insist that the teachers
should become better mathematicians. There is some justification in
this contention, but learning mathematics does not ensure that a
person will become a better teacher. Effort, time, and money have
been devoted to acquainting primary school teachers with the revised
mathematical content, and it could be asserted that teachers have not
benefited. Either the teachers have not grasped the information
sufficiently, or the efforts to acquaint them have been incorrect. The
psychological principles underlying the acquisition of mathematics
by children, and the place of mathematics in the primary school
curriculum have not been investigated thoroughly.

It is synonymous that changes in the teaching of mathematics have
accompanied changes in the primary school curriculum throughout
the past century. Such has occurred with the latest changes with the
introduction of the integrated day, vertical grouping, team teaching,
etc.; systems that encourage organizations and methods conducive to
individual learning. The question arises whether these forms of
teaching are too involved for all but the more able teachers. In the
attempts of some teachers to implement new curricula, mathematics
has lost its way. A teacher must systematize and organize her teaching
apart from how she is to systematize and organize the mathematics
within it. In their quest for security, many teachers have resorted to
commercial schemes of workbooks, workcards, or text books instead
of devising their own techniques for teaching mathematics. As a
result, their mathematics teaching is a veneer and children are not
given the opportunity to develop to their level of ability in
mathematics. Adopting this principle singles out mathematics from
the rest of the curriculum instead of it being an aspect around which

the primary school curriculum should revolve. The relevance of mathematics to children's learning is not taken into account. Teachers should become aware of the significance of mathematics in the curriculum. For example, in the teaching of reading, activities such as discrimination, generalization, comparisons, matching, grouping, straight and curved lines, etc. are used; all of which are mathematical in origin. The Bullock Report advocates a language policy across the curriculum. In view of the relevance of mathematics, a mathematics policy across the curriculum is worthy of consideration. Through their understanding of mathematics and its influence on other areas of learning, teachers will be able to apply this relevance to other areas of the curriculum. Mathematics treated in this way exercises in children the logical connections of patterns of relationship whereby they derive understanding of what they are doing.

A teacher's first responsibility is to pursue the aims of the school, and interpret these into classroom objectives. The teacher must stimulate learning and bring it about in a productive way, but some teachers are thwarted in their attempts to do this. The aims may be vague or unobtainable. The curriculum may not have been defined logically, and consist of meaningless exercises or a medley of unrelated parts. In circumstances such as these, initiative is drained from a teacher. She may have ambitions to teach with imagination and flair but these are reduced to the apathy that the curriculum instils. This state of affairs questions how the curriculum is being evaluated and what measures are used to assess the children. A system to test input/output of a school is an essential consideration of curriculum design, but it is frequently cast into the background or ignored. Irrespective of the approach to teaching in a school, evalution of the curriculum and assessment of children provide the head teacher and teachers with mechanisms to appraise the teaching and consider ways of improving it.

The competence of teachers is not the only factor to consider when examining mathematics and the primary school curriculum. 'Modern' or 'new' mathematics is often cited as the cause for 'falling standards'. There is no such thing as 'modern' or 'new' mathematics. The mathematics concerned has been practised for at least a century. All that is being attempted with the revised approach to mathematics teaching is to present the subject in an enlivened and interesting way for children to become involved instead of rejecting it as in the past. Perhaps, in the enthusiasm to make mathematics appealing, too much has been attempted. There is still a need for children to learn the basic processes of mathematics but these processes should be applied throughout learning.

Society, too, has its ideas on how children should be educated. Although it bestows authority to teachers to educate its children society has views on what it expects from children's attendance at school. In mathematics, the issue evolves into what society regards as mathematical competence. Does it wish to have children who are mechanically competent, or does it wish to have children who have developed a capability to think? The impression of school held by the majority of society was framed when they were pupils, and mathematics to them means arithmetic. But arithmetic is merely the manipulation of symbols in computation. Often facts are learned by rote and not understood. Society must appreciate that the situation has changed owing to the realization that mathematics is necessary to children if they are going to cope in life. Mathematics is essential to scientific, technological and economic development, but is also allows children to expand their landscapes by giving them awareness of how their world is constructed, and how man has used mathematics to adapt natural resources to suit his convenience.

The dissenters of present-day primary education argue that understanding by young children is a waste of time. They would prefer children to learn facts, and, once the facts have been acquired, hope that understanding materializes. This in many instances is a forlorn hope. Learning by dull and repetitive routines does not give incentive to understand, and this is what happened with so many children in mathematics. The subject became a bore and was dropped at the first opportunity. Moreover, it should be remembered that today's adult population are not as competent in mathematics as the 'back to basics' advocates would have us believe.

The contention is that not only primary school teachers but educationalists and society have failed to appreciate the role of mathematics in the education of young children. Mathematics is taken out of context with an emphasis on the subject for the subject's sake, and its relevance to the curriculum ignored. Proficiency in the basic skills of computation is essential for children to be able to perform adequately in other areas of curriculum content, but a danger exists of the 'back to basics' advocates taking the issue out of context. The press is not slow to latch on to any item of news that supports the 'basics ideal' to attack present-day teaching. Any research that suggests children are failing is given wide publicity, but often the research is biased with inadequate research design that does not account for vital factors. Occasionally, an article appears alleging that children do not know their tables, cannot multiply or divide but that they are experts at making things out of empty yoghourt pots, egg boxes and cornflake packets. The extent that this journalism gives a one-sided view can be measured by an extract (Hennessy 1978):

> My son is the victim of the fundamental misconception upon which all nursery education is based: that children learn primarily through play, that essential skills are acquired without teacher intervention and *teaching* is taboo.
>
> Somehow, magically, when the time was right, my son was supposed to lift his eyes up from the egg boxes and suddenly write, read, learn long division and know how to recite tables. The free-play fad was a reaction against rows of desks and ink-pots, and parrot fashion chanting.
>
> So classrooms buzzed with busily playing infants, the aggressive ones hogging the best toys and the timid ones snivelling in the corner with wooden jig-saw puzzles with half the pieces missing.
>
> Sadly there are limited employment prospects for the nation of cornflake packet artists we have reared under the free-play banner. Who wants to employ someone who has spent eight years sticking macaroni and dried beans on to cardboard and spraying them gold?

This account may have an element of truth in it, some teachers do not harness play to intellectual development, but children's emotional, social, and physical development need to be considered also, and play is a medium to cater for these. It is an exaggeration to allege that teaching is taboo. Although children have freedom to inquire and follow their own direction in play, they need help to translate what they are doing. This translation comes about by interpretation through language from a teacher. It cannot be denied that some children will repeat the play of previous occasions. This may be necessary for a short while as reinforcement, but constant repetition suggests the play being utilized for its own sake and not for learning. For play to facilitate learning, a teacher must be an active participant by acting as interpreter and guide when activities are in progress. The teacher must judge when to take an active role; when to stand back, when to interact, when to advise and when to interpret.

Teachers should become active associates in children's play. Their participation does not inhibit but enriches play, and specification of an active role is contrary to intervention. Intervention is used by many educationalists to pose the question, 'When should a teacher intervene in children's activities?' The term originates from the American pursual of behavioural objectives when children are put on stipulated paths of learning and the teacher intervenes at the correct moment to direct them to the ultimate goal. Intervention thereby could be misinterpreted by teachers, and its perpetuation has no respect for the act of teaching. Teachers teach, they do not intervene. Through their professional education and expertise, teachers become conscious of the appropriate times when to participate in learning. Intervention implies mediation and interrupting children in their activities and thought. Association means joining in with children to encourage a continuation of activities and thought.

To resort to an over-emphasis of computation skills in the primary school is a move that should be resisted. Primary school children should receive an education that will awaken them as human beings who are interested in the relevance of mathematics to their lives, are being led to come to terms with their world through mathematics, who use mathematics as a basic language to interpret and communicate with others, and who, through mathematics, are thinking in a logical and ordered way. This involves viewing mathematics realistically, and examining how it affects the primary school curriculum. When this has been accomplished, the onus is on schools to ensure that the principles are being carried out.

The task of providing children with a mathematical education is exacting for teachers, but it should not be abandoned for the easy way out of reverting to computation as the standard diet for primary schools. Teachers are taking the blame for the lack of qualities of excellence in mathematics, but on reflection are they to blame? If educationalists do not appreciate the role of mathematics in the primary school curriculum, and if society has not been acquainted with the fact, how can teachers be expected to teach children efficiently? After all, these are the two factions that teachers are trying to appease. The educationalists propound the theories for teachers to implement, and society receives the results of the practice.

REFERENCES

CHOAT, E. (1977). 'Primary Mathematics: The Challenge Ahead', *Ideas,* **37.** In *The New Era,* **58,** 5, 130-3.

HENNESSY, V. (1974, 14 August). 'Plight of the Cornflake Kids', *London Evening News.*

Chapter 1

The Influence of Mathematics on the Primary School Curriculum

A well known educationalist was heard to remark that study of primary mathematics teaching was of less value to teachers than a general appraisal of primary education. If asked to make a snap judgement, most people would agree, but when the matter is considered a less positive answer evolves. The educationalist probably based his decision on his own experience of learning mathematics. He was unaware, of the present approach to the teaching of mathematics in the primary school, and the influence of the subject on the curriculum.

No doubt, the educationalist thinks that mathematics in the primary school consists of practice in the operations on number. This is a false impression. Mathematics, as the science of space and number in the abstract to determine patterns of relationship, is implicit in almost everything in which primary school children are involved. As such, mathematics can be considered the foundation of learning for young children, and the subject around which the primary school curriculum revolves.

Curriculum theory has become a major study in education. Numerous books on curriculum have appeared in recent years, courses for teachers have arisen and higher degrees have been established, but most attention has been given to curricula in secondary schools and in higher education while study of the primary school curriculum has been relatively neglected (Choat 1974a). This is remarkable when the changes which have taken place in primary schools are considered. Not only has the content taught in primary schools changed dramatically but also the aims and objectives. The emphasis now is the education of persons by the recognition of each child as an individual, and teaching techniques have been revised to accommodate this.

Curriculum study attempts to rationalize the elements which constitute the curriculum. Curriculum aims, objectives, method, organization, evaluation, design, content, and innovation are examined theoretically, but rarely are the practical applications taken into account. Moreover, the function of mathematics in the primary school is seldom considered. Failure to do so is an omission for without mathematics the primary school curriculum would be non-existent.

The well-known educationalist will be astounded by this contention, but without mathematics children would not come to terms with life. A mathematical education awakens in children values which are essential to lead a full and active life as (a) mathematics has practical uses in an individual's activities of life; (b) mathematics is a cultural subject in its own right whereby an individual is led to come to terms with the world in which he lives; (c) mathematics is a part of an individual's basic language through which he is able to interpret and communicate with others; and, (d) involvement with, and deduction in, mathematics encourages logical and ordered thinking in an individual.

These values should be the aim of mathematics teaching in primary schools. Curriculum principles will not be interpreted by primary school teachers until they appreciate the relevance that these factors have on the curriculum. It cannot be otherwise if mathematics is everywhere and in almost everything. Teachers are unable to determine classroom relationships unless they rationalize possibilities for learning, are conscious of children's development in mathematics, are presenting challenge and avenues of inquiry for children to learn, and are aware of how mathematical knowledge is communicated between children and themselves. In short, a logic of the primary school curriculum is attained through the logic of teaching mathematics.

Education is the most powerful instrument possessed by society; its function being to organize, accelerate, and direct the process of learning to produce individuals who will contribute to the fitness of society. In this context, society cannot make demands unless it is sufficiently educated itself to acknowledge the magnitude of the demands. Schools should be framed and conducted to meet the future social and practical wants, but such is not feasible as society is unable to foretell its needs of ten years hence. An estimation of possible requirements may be forecast, but there is no guarantee of accuracy. As a compromise, schools have abided by doctrines which contend that education can be conceived as life itself. Curriculum policies and plans emanating from such a notion are formulated to meet immediate needs and problems of society and individuals. Consequently, educational change is perpetuated by social utility; when change is convenient to the existing social pattern.

Social utility has controlled the curriculum since the Education Act, 1870. The development of industrialization in the nineteenth century created a need for skilled workers. When factories grew in size and complexity, a demand arose for more clerical workers and minor professionals. Forced by these necessities, and restricted by the notorious system of 'payment by results', purposeful education was seen as what was useful for the sons and daughters of the working class. Its aim was the conquest of illiteracy through a curriculum limited to formal studies with children learning by heart and complying to silence, orderliness, and conformity to rule. The emphasis of the curriculum was children's attainment in reading, writing, and arithmetic.

Arithmetic was organized on class lines with extreme thoroughness. Text-books were few, closely printed, and packed with lengthy and involved examples. They were written for teachers rather than for children, and their authors assumed that teachers would give elaborate oral demonstrations and detailed explanations of each new stage of learning. In most instances, the examples were dictated by teachers or copied by children from the blackboard. The value placed on prowess in arithmetic was so great that almost half the school day was given to working exercises, the transcription of figures from the blackboard, or listening to explanations of how answers had been obtained (Fleming 1946, pp.39-58).

Although some enlightened Infants' Schools adopted more enterprising approaches by implementing teaching based on the doctrines of Froebel and Montessori, education in most schools remained geared to the principle of rote learning in English, history, geography, arithmetic, etc. for the next seventy odd years. Not until the Hadow Report (1931) did educational change attract attention. Influenced by the philosophy of Dewey and the psychology of Burt, the Hadow Report did much to shape the future of primary education, but it was some years before its recommendations took effect. The Report suggested that the difference in intellectual capacity between the brightest and less able children made it necessary to classify a single age-group in several sections (streaming) by the age of ten years, but the most memorable recommendation was for the curriculum to be thought of in terms of activity and experience rather than knowledge to be acquired and facts to be stored.

The Hadow Report's (ibid pp.80, 139-45) references to mathematics were confusing. While stressing that too much time was given to arithmetic and complaining that too little attention was given to the study of simple geometry, the Report insisted that primary schools should be concerned mainly with the fundamental processes or 'rules' of arithmetic. It contended, 'that these fundamental processes of arithmetic shall become automatic before the child leaves the primary school'. The Report maintained that unless a child could add, subtract, multiply and divide accurately, quickly and without hestitation, his future progress would be severely handicapped. Clear thinking was seen as essential in arithmetic and, although a child should know how tables of multiplication are constructed and be able to build the 'sixteen times' table when required, the capability was no substitute for the rote-knowledge of the ordinary tables.

The complexity of the Hadow Report is best illustrated with its view on the use of mathematics in the environment and, conversely, its castigation of practical activities in arithmetic. 'From the first, increasing attention should be paid to the applications of arithmetic to matters within the children's environment', it states. Home experiences were recommended for dealing with shape, size, weight and money so that children might become conversant with geometrical properties and learn the associated words. Nevertheless, the Report added, 'it has often been urged that the beginnings of arithmetic should be 'concrete'. . . if this means that the child must only deal with articles and never with number in the abstract, must add horses to horses and take nuts from nuts, and never add three to four or take seven from twelve, it is pure pedantry . . . the truth is that the fundamental operations of addition, subtraction, multiplication and division belong to the abstract side of mathematics and are most simply and effectively dealt with in the abstract.

No wonder that the Hadow Report had little immediate effect, and, even after the Education Act, 1944, curriculum reform was practically non-existent. The principle of giving every child a secondary education accentuated existing practices of primary schools. With the majority of places at 'selective' secondary schools free, the aim of most junior schools was to secure as many places as possible in these schools for their children. Streaming was imposed and an emphasis was placed on reading, writing and arithmetic to prepare the children for the qualifying examination known as the eleven-plus.

In no area of the curriculum was the intention more noticeable than in mathematics. Wheatley (1977) diagnosed the content of the eleven-plus examination in Essex over a period of twenty-five years. From 1937 until 1962 there was little change in the examination with (i) addition, subtraction, multiplication, and division of number, money, and length, (ii) long division and long multiplication, (iii) area, and (iv) fractions, as the stable items. The similarities did not end there. Question 1 consisted of a number of simple, mental sums. The next seven questions on each paper were equally alike in format year after year.

The eleven-plus dictated what was taught in schools. There was little attempt to teach anything mathematical except what would appear on the test paper. Wheatley *(ibid)* adds that even when the examiners altered a question to discover mathematical 'flair', teachers negated it by drilling children to achieve a correct answer. He illustrates this by quoting question 9(d) of the 1962 Essex eleven-plus paper:

> Fifteen thousand people paid for admission to a football match and £1,350 was taken in gate money. Adults paid 2 shillings but children were admitted at half price. How many of the people were children?

The question often appeared with different priced stamps as the basis of the problem, and was referred to as a 'stamp sum' by teachers. Children were taught the knack of how to obtain correct answers, and many hours of teaching were involved.

Two factors hastened curriculum reform in primary schools — the launching of the Russian Sputnik in 1957, and the spread of comprehensive education after 1965. The Sputnik was evidence of Russia's scientific development, and a warning to the western world that they had to keep abreast of scientific and technological development. Some local education authorities had adopted comprehensive schools but the full impetus of reform did not materialize until the Labour Government took office in 1965. Pledging equal educational opportunity for all, Circular 10/65 was issued and each local authority was requested to submit plans for the re-organization of secondary education on comprehensive lines. Many LEAs re-organized quickly, and the eleven-plus disappeared from junior schools. This cast a new horizon for primary education. Many schools which were streamed previously soon adopted non-streaming. The work of Piaget on how children learn was gaining momentum. To meet the technological demand, mathematics was taking a new direction with revised ideas of what constituted mathematics, and the nature of mathematical reasoning. Allied to these changes, the philosophy of activity, discovery, and experience as expounded by Dewey was attracting attention and new organizations and methods such as projects, topics, centres of interest, integrated day, team teaching, and individual learning were introduced into primary education.

It was not surprising that the primary school curriculum underwent major revision. The traditional ways of teaching were abandoned for techniques which attempted to cater for the acquisition of knowledge through child-centredness. In many primary schools, a fixed set of subjects and a time-table no longer existed. The organization of the school day and curriculum content were left entirely to teachers' discretions. Children were able to pursue endless subjects from geology to cartography. These primary schools were allowed to adopt illogical principles and meander through a maze with some Head Teachers and classroom practitioners selecting innovations that they did not understand but which they adopted so as to be in fashion. Other schools curbed their enthusiasm and analysed the consequences before attempting change. These schools operated a learner-centred approach with a curriculum that had purpose.

It can be seen that these changes in the primary school curriculum coincided with changes in mathematical content. Previously what was taught in arithmetic was straightforward and teachers coped adequately. The remainder of their teaching fitted into a neat format, and the organizations and methods were equally as simple. But this did not mean that children were being educated. With instruction the prerogative, children were indoctrinated in what teachers believed they should learn irrespective of whether the children understood what they were learning.

Acquiring mathematics through understanding was accompanied by mathematics which the majority of teachers had not encountered previously. Sets, symmetry, multi-base, probability, graphs, etc. were as foreign to teachers as were pre-operational stage, concrete operations, concepts, etc. Thus, many teachers found difficulty in coming to terms with the new teaching techniques, and with the mathematics.

Some people now express disillusion with children's attainment in primary schools, and a parallel can be drawn through mathematics. The dissenters wish children to learn basic skills by which they mean rote learning of the operations on number — addition, subtraction, multiplication and division. This entails a return to the traditional ways of teaching with mathematics practised as in the days of the eleven-plus. Instead of preparing children for the examination, teachers will concentrate on teaching rules and ways of reaching answers to sums. Attention to children as individuals, and to mathematical development through concept acquisition will fall by the wayside, and much of the practical work which enables this will be discarded. With a more formal approach to mathematics there is a likelihood that the remainder of the primary school curriculum will formalize also. With children restricted to their desks to 'do sums', less movement within classrooms will be encouraged to undertake projects and other activities which involve inquiry. In other words, the primary school curriculum will lose flair, and the loss of flair will encourage rigidity.

This situation need not come about if teachers provide answers from their classrooms. Mathematics and the primary school curriculum must be determined logically if teachers are to rationalize what they are hoping to achieve. There is also the question of evaluation. Thereby, the exercise requires thought; organized thought by logical method.

Logic, properly used, does not shackle thought but gives it freedom and boldness. Illogical thought hesitates to draw conclusions because it never knows what it means, what it assumes, how far it trusts its assumptions or what the effect will be on any modification of assumptions. The fundamental basis of this relevant logic is to ponder with an active mind over the known facts which have been directly observed (Whitehead 1932, pp. 175-9).

How can logic be applied to mathematics and the primary school curriculum, and how necessary is it? Mathematics teaching and a curriculum which have not been logically deduced dissolve into meaningless exercises or collections of unassembled parts without ultimate aims. There are no directions for teachers to follow. Terminologies are accepted at face value without consideration of intended outcomes. Mathematics teaching and the curriculum become aimless muddles. Contrary to this are mathematics teaching and a primary school curriculum with definite directions. Conclusions are drawn because teachers know what is meant and what is intended. Teachers can trust the assumptions as these have been considered rationally and because a framework exists. Modifications are possible to enhance what is being attempted, and to secure more definite and refined aims. The mathematics teaching and curriculum have been constructed for a particular school and the children in it. Frequently the latter aspect is overlooked with curricula constructed to suit academic ideals instead of the needs of children. Curriculum content becomes the over-riding emphasis, and in mathematics a situation evolves whereby children are fitted to mathematics instead of fitting mathematics to children.

Primary school teachers should reason why they are teaching mathematics and, likewise, define how they will teach the subject. When these have been resolved, they will be able to apply logical reasoning to other areas of the curriculum. Having decided their aims, objectives, organizations, methods, and means of evaluation of mathematics teaching, they will institute the principles into their teaching generally. This implies that a school will have a philosophy of what it is attempting to achieve, and which gives rise to certain aims that can be broken down into specified objectives, and a teaching programme for securing these objectives. The objectives need to be considered from a psychological stance, i.e. how children learn, levels of development, language development, factors which may cause emotional stress, and the sociological implications, etc. if children are to attain degrees of excellence in learning.

Kerr (1968, pp. 11-37) refers to the curriculum as all learning which is planned and guided by the school whether it is carried out in groups, individually, as a class, or inside or outside the school, and suggests that it be divided into four inter-related components — objectives, knowledge, learning experiences, and evaluation. Kerr is aligning with Bloom (1956) and Krathwohl (1964) when they define knowledge, comprehension, application, analysis, synthesis and evaluation as the taxonomies of educational objectives. Gribble (1970, pp. 56-8), while acknowledging Bloom as an influential person on curriculum theory, criticizes Bloom's definition of educational objectives as being divided into two main categories — 'knowledge', and 'skills and ability'. Gribble alleges that Bloom refers to knowledge as remembering or recalling facts, principles and methods

— activities which are purely rote — while comprehending, applying and analysing are skills or capabilities which are not essential to knowing. But, Gribble suggests, mental abilities and skills are part of what is involved in knowing something for knowing something involves judging that something is so, and judgement is a complex mental operation. Capabilities and skills are not separable from knowing something for they are unable to be specified or described independently of the various forms of knowledge. To attribute ability, skill or conceptualization to a child, his performance should reach certain specifications by which required qualities may be checked (Choat 1977). Gribble maintains that there is nothing wrong with saying that someone is capable of making judgements, or that he is exercising mental skills such as comprehension, analysis or synthesis and so on in doing so. The problem is that so little is being said unless the particular criteria which differentiates one kind of analysis, and one kind of synthesis from another is referred to. A further danger arises when capabilities, skills, and conceptualizations are spoken about without differentiating them, and with the implication that skill at analysis or synthesis in one form of knowledge is transferred to another. Although skilled in one form of critical analysis, there is no guarantee of carry-over for a child to possess undifferentiated analytical ability.

There is a need to consider why certain things are taught in the primary school, and the purpose of the curriculum. Clearly, one aim is to offer experiences to children that, through conceptualization, will develop understanding to cope sensibly with life. A deeper purpose is that the curriculum should explain to children their world and to achieve this they are dependent on mathematics. This implies starting with children themseleves — the making use of their own body movements, the environment which surrounds them, how man has discovered and used the world's resources, and how they interpret and communicate their findings. These qualities originate through children's investigations of space — how they adapt, manipulate, and control it — and align with the values mentioned previously that accrue from a mathematical education. If primary school children are to be educated, the curriculum should be designed to recognize them as individuals, with those principles postulated by Wood (1940) acting as the inspiration:

> The curriculum is educationally effective to the degree
> that it recognizes: (a) that the individual is an active agent

in the learning process, and (b) that the individual's ever-expanding environment is the proper source of new meanings or content.

The primary school curriculum should be all embracing with children no longer obedient to learn facts dictated by the teacher, and expected to acquire skills by endless repetition. Strategies within the curriculum should be devised to provide for (a) a need to belong, (b) a need for activity, (c) a need for curiosity, and (d) a need to be challenged (Choat and Lasenby, 1972). Only when mathematics becomes exciting to children will a teacher be able to claim that she is able to offer them a 'relevant' mathematical education (Choat, 1974b). Then she may justifiably say that they are interested in the relevance of mathematics to life; that they are using their ability to ask questions, interpret their actions, and communicate their experiences; that they are concerned with the patterns, relationships, perceptions and representations of their world; and that they have the tenacity and will to further their inquiries.

This learner-centred approach does not mean adoption of a *laissez faire* attitude to the exclusion of systematization, structure and logic in the primary school curriculum. The abiding features were enumerated by Hirst (1969) when he explained:

There are three closely related elements in curriculum planning. 1. Objectives as a result of teaching; qualities of mind, knowledge, skills, and values that we wish pupils to acquire. 2. A programme of activities and work, the plan of what we as teachers, and our pupils as learners, do to achieve these objectives. 3. Content or subject matter of these activities to reach the objectives.

From this diagnosis of mathematics and the primary school fundamental considerations emerge. First, there is a need for a framework within which teachers are able to implement learning situations for children to reach desired objectives. Second, there is the recognition of the importance of sequence which Richmond (1968, p.194) describes as (a) in the sense of ensuring that the inherent logic of the subject matter, task, or discipline is followed, and (b) in the sense of ensuring that both the teaching and learning processes keep step with children's psychological levels of development.

When implementing the curriculum, a teacher must bear in mind that learning is a continuous process. Children vary in capability, and in the extent that their attitude to learning is affected by social, emotional, physical and intellectual factors. Irrespective of divergencies, a teacher's task is to provide stimulation and opportunities that will motivate children to learn. To achieve this, teachers depend upon their initial and in-service training, and experience acquired in the execution of their task. This 'know-how' is related to individual observations of children to assess needs comparable to each child's level of development and pace of learning.

Schools are established to educate the young, and a successful school will have carefully and logically defined its curriculum. The traditional approach in primary schools relies upon authoritarian principles. Teachers are the acknowledged leaders who decide everything while the children are submissive to the teachers' whims. An active, challenging, inquiring, understanding, 'mathematically inspired' primary education depends upon teacher association based on reciprocal personal relationships. Teachers are active participants in whatever form the curriculum may take.

Although children may have freedom to be active and to inquire, they need assistance to translate actions and this comes about by communication and interpretation through language from teachers. Teachers must judge when to take an active role in any learning situation, when to stand back, when to interact, when to advise, and when to interpret. Teachers become active associates in children's learning. This is in contrast to a rejection of traditional orthodoxy only to replace it with a system which has no curriculum principles and which encourages teachers to adopt an 'anything goes' attitude. Teachers have a responsibility to maintain levels of expectation and to require qualities of excellence from children. To comply with such exacting demands through a mathematically inspired curriculum in the primary school is not easy, but only when teachers realize the influence which mathematics has on the curriculum will children be equipped to meet the requirements of society.

REFERENCES

BLOOM, B.S., *et al.* (1956). *Taxonomy of Educational Objectives: Handbook I, The Cognitive Domain.* London: Longman.

CHOAT, E. (1974a) 'Curriculum Design in the Primary School'. *Forum for the Discussion of New Trends in Education,* **17**, 1, 15-7.

CHOAT, E. (1974b). 'Johnnie is Disadvantaged; Johnnie is Backward. What Hope for Johnnie?' *Mathematics Teaching,* **69**, pp. 9-13.

CHOAT, E. (1977 18 March) 'Standards or Stipulations in Primary Mathematics'. *The Times Educational Supplement.*

CHOAT, E. and LAZENBY, M. (1972). 'The Curriculum and Disadvantaged Children', Paper 11, presented to Social Deprivation and Change in Education Conference. University of York.

FLEMING, C.M. (1946). *Research and the Basic Curriculum.* London: University of London Press.

GRIBBLE, J. (1970). *Introduction to Philosophy of Education.* Boston: Allyn & Bacon.

HIRST, P.H. (1969) 'The Logic of the Curriculum', *The Journal of Curriculum Studies,* **1**, 2, 142-58.

KERR, J.F. (1968). 'The Problems of Curriculum Reform'. In: KERR J.F. (Ed) *Changing the Curriculum.* London: University of London Press.

KRATHWOHL, D.R., *et al.* (1964). *Taxonomy of Educational Objectives: Handbook II, The Affective Domain.* London: Longman.

RICHMOND, W.K. (1968). *Readings in Education.* London: Methuen.

The Report of the CONSULTATIVE COMMITTEE ON THE PRIMARY SCHOOL, (The Hadow Report) (1931). London: HMSO.

WHEATLEY, D. (1977) 'Mathematical Concepts and Language 1937-1977', *The New Era,* **58**, 5,, 134-7.

WHITEHEAD, A.N. (1932) *The Aims of Education.* London: Benn.

WOOD, H.B. (1940) 'The School Curriculum and Community Life', *Commonwealth Review,* **21**, 5.

Chapter 2
Disagreements on the Teaching of Mathematics in the Primary School

Jane, a 'rising five', began school after the Easter holiday. During the summer holiday, her mother was eager to relate how well Jane had done. She had begun to read, could write her name, and the numerals — 1, 2, 3, 4, and 5. The school was further commended. Her mother heard the children reciting the numbers 'one to a hundred' when waiting to collect Jane.

This is a typical reaction from a parent to a child's performance in school. The child is showing evidence of what she is doing and is achieving in the three Rs. But is the evidence as conclusive as it appears to Jane's mother?

I was interested in the references to mathematics. For a child, not yet five years old, to be monologuing from one to a hundred appeared absurd, but why was she symbolizing one, two, three, four and five? Did she understand the symbols, and could she apply them with understanding?

I called to Jane, and took objects which were near at hand; these being five pencils and five one pence coins. The objects were arranged in a Piagetian one-to-one correspondence check, i.e.

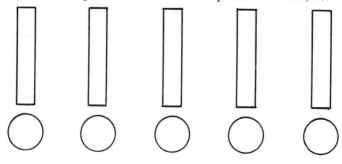

'Tell me', I said to Jane, 'are there more pencils, more pennies, or the same amount of pencils and pennies?'

'More pencils', she replied without hesitation.

With Jane watching, I readjusted the pennies for the arrangement to become:

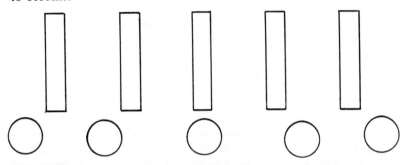

'Now, what do you think?' I asked Jane.

'More pennies', was her immediate answer.

Jane was at the stage of global comparison only. She made no attempt to assess the situation. Although the items were units, Jane had not reached the stage of counting the pencils, and then the pennies, to determine their respective numerical values. Her reaction was to guess with the first check (probably the larger size of the pencils attracted her attention), while the length clue influenced her with the second check. Moreover, her change from pencils for the first check to pennies for the second check indicated a lack of connection between the two checks; although she had not witnessed any pennies removed.

What will happen to Jane now? Her mother is aware of the situation regarding number, and she should give Jane activities which will aid development in 'numberness'. In school, Jane will have no option but to continue to 'learn', mathematics in the way her teacher feels is appropriate and, on the evidence of the past term, will most likely be doing addition by the end of next term. Whether she understands what she is doing is another matter, but the approach to mathematics in Jane's school is approved in many quarters.

How children should learn mathematics has been given attention in The Great Debate, national newspapers, and educational journals. Often, the divergence is regarded as a dispute between 'modern' and 'traditional' views, but this is not the whole issue. The disagreement is deeper than beliefs in teaching approaches and is more an argument on what mathematics is being learned and how it is being learned. The assumption held by many in post-primary education is that mathematics, as taught in several primary schools, is not a suitable preparation in mathematics. This is because the schools are following a principle of children learning mathematics with understanding. The advocates of the method respond by contending that children who understand do not need to rely on rote learning when the subject is taught logically, and when reasoning reveals the inherent subject matter.

The severity of disapproval of 'learning with understanding' is such that Kline (1973) can devote a whole book to its condemnation. He argues (p.49) that a concentration on the deductive approach omits vital work, and destroys the life and spirit of mathematics. He also alleges (pp. 58-9) that some curriculum makers confuse what is logically prior with what is logically desirable while others, seeking novelty, fasten on to rigour. Kline maintains that the simple topics of elementary mathematics are taken and made to appear profound by cloaking them in what can be described as 'prissy pedantry' while giving the impression of deep mathematical insight. He further remarks (pp. 101-2) that items such as bases and inequalities were removed from the levels at which they were taught previously with no gain, or reason to question, and that set theory, matrices, and abstract algebra were chosen to show that the curriculum has caught up with advances in mathematics; although these advances have no proper place or function for young children. 'New' mathematics as a whole, Kline adds, is a presentation of the shallow mathematician who appreciates only petty deductive details and minor pedantic, sterile distinctions such as between number and numeral and who seeks to enhance trivia with imposing sounding terminology and symbolism. The stress of final, sophisticated versions of simple ideas, while treating the deeper ideas superficially, assumes a dogmatic character. According to Kline, this approach leads to an erosion of the vitality of mathematics, authoritarian teaching, and rote learning of new routines far more useless than the traditional routines. Consequently it presents form at the expense of substance, and substance without pedagogy.

Referring to the USA, Kline (pp. 119-43) adds, the leaders of curriculum reform in mathematics have been professors who, because they have no idea of the role that mathematics has played in history, are ignorant as mathematicians and are uneducated human beings. When called upon to assist in the preparation of curricula, these professors suggest the narrow, specialized abstract topics with which they are familiar and, making concessions for the elementary level, suggest watered-down versions of the more sophisticated treatments of 'traditional' mathematics. Having become wise through the acquisition of a PhD., and possibly a prestigous position at a university, they believe themselves experts in areas in which they are totally ignorant. Forgetting that they required years to reach their level of understanding, they believe their knowledge can be imparted immediately to young minds. Furthermore, their interest is to develop future mathematics but, because they fail to consider teaching, the professional mathematicians are the most serious threat to the teaching of mathematics.

The objectives of education must be determined before curricula can be prepared appropriate to children's development. Thought should be given to education as a whole before objectives are finalized, and this, Kline contends, mathematicians will not do. He claims that most mathematicians are not interested in the psychology of learning as it is a more difficult subject than mathematics. Mathematicians will not take the trouble to find out what psychology can offer, nor will they take the trouble to develop their own skills in the art of teaching.

Kline's comments are reported in length. They are scathing of learning with understanding, but there is truth in his references to rationalization of objectives and the role of psychology in the learning of mathematics. The view held previously had objectives — for children to acquire proficiency in the operations on number — but it disregarded psychology. On the other hand, many people now claim that learning with understanding has given too much weight to psychology and disregarded objectives. The failure to reconcile objectives and psychology, and to recognize how they influence teaching, is the wedge between primary schools and post-primary institutions, and is the cause of mathematics teaching having lost its way.

The objectives in the two sections of education appear to be in opposition. This is emphasized by Hancox (1974) who claims that many students in Further Education use 'modern' mathematics as an excuse for a lack of arithmetical skills and that they are devoid of 'numeracy'. Hancox claims that to these students the 'how' of mathematics is more important than the 'why'. He alleges that very few children in primary schools now recite the tables of multiplication and asks whether understanding the tables is better than learning them. 'Better for the able pupils may be, but why should not the majority learn their tables "parrot fashion" at a time when a child likes repetition and reciting tables', Hancox contends.

Hancox's assertions are presumptuous. Learning tables by rote does not ensure that children can use them. Knowledge of the tables is essential, but a knowledge which can be applied in situations other than in which they have been learned. Of equal concern is the assumption that young children enjoy repeating and reciting tables. Understanding was encouraged because of ignorance, boredom and frustration brought about by dragooning tables into children. Apparently, Hancox has no primary school teaching experience. He has never been through the drudgery of trying to 'teach' tables to a class of less able children; the very pupils he is proposing should be taught by rote. Even when tables have been learned, it is difficult for these children to apply them in the most simple situations. Hancox's attitude is an example of the failure to appreciate psychological principles, and is exemplified when he ridicules the Chinese proverb quoted in the Nuffield Guides:

> I hear, and I forget
> I see, and I remember
> I do, and I understand

'If the children "do" they will understand but this is rarely the case. The children cannot do arithmetic, and hence they cannot hope to understand it', Hancox claims.

Levy (1976a), a secondary school teacher with primary school experience, contends that failure in mathematics lies in the infants' and junior schools because of low expectations. He feels that the downward trend can be reversed by putting children back to carefully structured daily work for practice in the basic skills of arithmetic, and to learn the table facts and number bonds by heart. There is confusion with what Levy means by structure. Structure to him implies stipulated learning tasks followed in a specific sequence, whereas its more orthodox use is to refer to organization arrangements. Carefully structured organization is both desirable and essential for, without precise planning, no teacher is able to teach efficiently. To know the tables of multiplication and number bonds by heart are necessary objectives in mathematics, but how are they achieved? Once children have acquired the underlying concepts, they can apply their understanding to facilitate memory of the principles and combinations of numbers. Understanding, to Levy (1976b), is a further area of conflict. In reply to an article by Choat (1976), he intimates that he would take issue with anyone who set out to teach a process without first making an honest attempt at understanding but, later, decries the implication that 'teaching the use of a process must wait until understanding has been achieved is a dangerous nonsense'.

Disillusion of learning mathematics with understanding, and the blame on the primary school, have been dealt with in depth to allow the gulf which exists to be appreciated. Two issues evolve (a) dissatisfaction with the way young children are taught mathematics, and (b) young children are not learning what the critics feel is appropriate mathematics but, it should be remembered, those concerned have vested interests in mathematics and ultimate aims for their pupils to attain examination successes in the subject. Throughout their deliberations, the emphasis is on mathematics (objectives), and no mention is made of children as individuals (psychology). Mathematics comes to them easily, and they are unable to appreciate why others fail to capture its magnetism. Engrossed in their subject, they lack knowledge of the broader aspects of education; particularly developmental factors which influence mathematical learning, and the principles of the primary school curriculum. The consequences are rigid expectations in mathematics for children leaving primary school.

It cannot be denied that some primary school teachers are confused, and insecure in their teaching of mathematics. Sympathy can be extended to these teachers; sympathy which is appreciated by those who have taught in primary schools. Primary school teachers are not concerned with mathematics only. They have had many changes to contend with in recent years. The philosophy of primary education has changed, with an emphasis on children as individuals and this has encouraged mixed ability teaching. New schools have been built on the open-plan principle instead of enclosed classrooms. This has encouraged new forms of teaching organizations such as team teaching, vertical grouping, integrated day, etc. New subjects such as science and a second language, and different approaches to teaching, such as centres of interest and projects, which encourage integration of curriculum content, have been introduced and take some of the time allocated previously to traditional subjects. Emphasis on language development and 'standards' of reading have occupied teachers' attention and time in recent years. To cope with these changes, teachers must attain efficiency and organize effectively before children can learn profitably.

Attempts have been made to assist primary school teachers with their teaching of mathematics. Local education authorities have issued guidelines, numerous books explaining the theoretical principles and text books providing schemes in mathematics have been published, structural apparatus has proliferated, research into the acquisition of mathematics has published findings, and in-service courses have been available. If these efforts have not produced secure teachers of mathematics the reason for failure, if it exists, must be elsewhere.

It is suggested in some quarters that primary mathematics teaching will never be satisfactory because a number of primary school teachers do not have GCE O-levels in mathematics. The implication is inefficient teaching, but this is not necessarily true. Many teachers who had difficulty with mathematics appreciate the problems confronting the children they teach. Aware of their own inadequacies, a large number of primary school teachers have devoted time and effort to apply themselves to something which previously they had rejected, and have become good teachers of the subject. A teacher's outlook is the criterion for determining her teaching. Satisfactory results are obtained only by enthusiastic and able teachers who may use different teaching techniques to secure the same results, but even the best techniques will fail with uninspired and incapable teachers. Bruner may say that any subject can be taught effectively in some intellectually, honest form to any child, but the retort is, 'Can it be taught by any teacher?'.

Teachers may claim that they have only a small contribution to make to a child's education, the greatest influence being that of parents. If so, why are children compulsorily sent to school? Acknowledging that much of a child's learning takes place in the pre-school years, that books are available, and that the BBC TV series 'You and Me' assists parents by providing examples of early mathematical experiences, many parents are mathematically inadequate, and even those who are competent are confused by revised teaching techniques. Some primary schools have made efforts to acquaint parents with the mathematics in their school but, whatever the implications, the responsibility for children's attainment in mathematics lies with teachers. Unless teachers are prepared to provide the stimulation, children will be devoid of motivation in mathematics.

The prime concern of teachers should be the school's aims and objectives, and how these relate to individual children. The task is two-fold in mathematics — (a) preparing those children who will become mathematicians and apply their specialized knowledge in industry, commerce, management, and teaching, and (b) preparing other children to a degree of competence in mathematics for use and pleasure in their ordinary lives. The extent to which children aspire in either direction depends on the psychological factors of intelligence and the ability to abstract, but teaching and learning are influenced by a teacher's awareness of how children acquire mathematics, factors likely to retard mathematical development, features related to mathematical progression, presentation of learning, and the uses of mathematics. These aspects warrant as much consideration as the content to be taught. Implicit within these prerogatives is the distinction between 'understanding' and 'rote learning'.

Skemp (1976) specifies two categories of understanding in mathematics — relational understanding and instrumental understanding. Relational understanding is not only knowing what to do but why as it includes rationalization of the underlying mathematical relationships and properties. Instrumental understanding is when pupils and teachers think that they understand something if they are able to obtain correct answers to a given category of questions without knowing why the method works.

Are two subjects, relational mathematics and instrumental mathematics, being considered when mathematics teaching is debated? The subject matter may be the same but the resulting two kinds of knowledge are different. In Skemp's view, there is a strong case for regarding them as different kinds of mathematics and, if this distinction is accepted, mathematics is a false friend for many children as they find to their cost.

There is an emphasis in post-primary education for instrumental mathematics whereas many primary schools favour relational mathematics. But what of the primary schools that favour instrumental mathematics? Jane attends such a school, and her capability to acquire relational mathematics is not being explored. This implies that a child's attitude towards mathematics, and her prowess in the subject, is determined by the type of mathematics teaching which she encounters.

If all is not well with teaching, there is only one set of sufferers, the pupils subjected to the teaching. There is a need to determine how continuity can be established between educational establishments, viz.

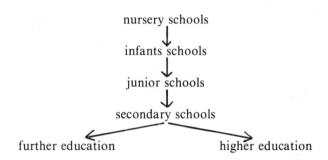

Until this is accomplished, the teaching of mathematics will remain under dispute. Mathematical education begins in the early years, and is a continuous process throughout life. For individual teachers and schools to foster their own ideals and disregard others is open to question. How will Jane fare if her next teacher follows a different teaching approach, or if she is removed to another school which practises a different philosophy?

This does not imply a common curriculum in mathematics. Answers will not be found until psychologically sound reasons are resolved for teaching in particular ways. Competent teaching of mathematics requires a knowledge of the subject, awareness of how this knowledge is relevant to children, expertise in knowing how the knowledge can be presented for children to acquire relational understanding and skill in developing situations and circumstances to allow the knowledge to be presented, while taking into account that each child is an individual with different needs, attitudes and levels of progression.

Mathematics requires children to think, and to explore and investigate the situations of life and concrete facts. Mathematics is basic to life in nature, the landscape, construction, manufacture, play, and ordinary events. Space surrounds man and it is natural that he should investigate how he can adapt it for use. Mathematics is the key to understanding the physical world and has given man the conviction that he can fathom the secrets of nature. Knowledge is a whole and mathematics a part of that whole. Mathematics did not develop apart from other activities and interests. The relationship of mathematics to other human interests should be integral to the objectives of mathematics teaching.

The aim of mathematics teaching, should be to develop in children a capability to come to terms with the world in which they live by seeing, appreciating and using the aesthetic qualities which mathematics gives to life, and use the relationships, concepts and skills of mathematics to cope with what they will encounter. If mathematics develops these attributes in children, reasons exist for a more thorough appraisal of the educational theory which underlies the teaching of mathematics. It is simple to state that such and such should be taught, but 'why' is it taught, 'how' is it taught, and 'what' are the best forms of teaching method and organization?

REFERENCES

CHOAT, E. (1976). 'Mathematics — Not a Tin of Beans', *ILEA Contact*, **5,** 12, 25-6.
HANCOX, D. (1974, 22 February). 'On the Battleground of Modern Mathematics', *The Times Educational Supplement*, p.22.
KLINE, M. (1973) *Why Johnny Can't Add*, New York: St. Martin's Press.
LEVY, A. (1976a). 'Low Expectations', *ILEA Contact*, **5,** 9, 20-1.
LEVY, A. (1976b), 'Understanding a Process', letter to *ILEA Contact*, **5, 14.**
SKEMP, R.R. (1976). 'Relational Understanding and Instrumental Understanding', *Mathematics Teaching*, **77,** pp.20-6,

Chapter 3
Understanding in Mathematics

A child building a tower is a common sight in nursery and infants schools, but the activity could be initiated in several ways. The task may originate from a teacher with a desire for a child to acquire knowledge of the properties of blocks, by the child through his inquisitiveness to do things with the blocks, or by mathematical insight through an intention to construct. Consequently, an onlooker is likely to witness any of the following scenes in a classroom.

1. The teacher merely describes that the largest block is placed at the bottom and the other blocks are added according to their reduction in size.

2. The teacher builds the tower in seriation while the child watches.

3. The teacher takes the largest block, says it is the base of the tower, and asks the child to complete the task.

4. The child is given assorted blocks and asked to build a tower.

5. The child is given assorted blocks and allowed to do what he wishes with them. He places the blocks on top of each other, and when the task is completed realizes that he has built a tower.

6. The child intends to build a tower. He rationalizes that he must begin with the largest block and seriate the remaining blocks in order of size.

The manner in which an activity is undertaken determines the kind of experience for a child. Obviously, a single experience is insufficient to acquire understanding as repetition is necessary, but children's understanding from an experience is liable to vary.

Skemp (1976) drew attention to two interpretations of understanding in mathematics — relational understanding and instrumental understanding — and the connotations attached to these definitions have a significant bearing on the way children's mathematical competence is assessed. Are children assessed in mathematics for knowing what they are doing, or are they assessed for being able to do without knowing? The level at which children understand must reflect the way they have learned. Moreover, understanding should not be confused with skill. Skill is the ability to perform a set routine, and requires a period of experiment and practice by trial and error before the routine is carried out smoothly and efficiently. A skill may be performed with relational understanding or instrumental understanding.

Rote learning is trusting to memory facts which are not related to existing knowledge so facts are without assimilation to existing schema (Skemp, 1971, p.51). Symbol manipulations are memorized and the degree to which many able children memorize is remarkable. The appearance of learning mathematics is maintained until a stage is reached when only concept acquisition will suffice. The learner then attempts to master new tasks by the only means he knows — memorization of rules. This being impossible, even the outward appearance of success ceases, and with distress the child falls by the wayside. This has happened to many adults and, unless rectified, could happen to Jane. Conditioned to rote learning and trusting to memory, an individual is unable to rationalize relationships inherent in mathematics. The mathematics appears beyond him so it is not attempted, and he falls back to the excuse that he is no good at mathematics. If, instead, the situation is broken down into logical stages and begun at the foundation stage, the individual is free to proceed through the stages to form concepts and acquire relational understanding.

The environment is vital to children's mathematical development as they live in a series of situations that it creates, and the interaction with these situations constitutes experience. During this interaction of activities and explorations, concepts are formed. Consequently, children's educators (parents and teachers) are responsible for determining the environment and, subsequently, the experiences which children acquire. Nevertheless, concept formation is not an automatic process. Gathering and piecing together experiences are possible through perception, but perception is not a casual survey of the environment. It is diagnosing the objects that constitute the environment through sight, sound, taste, touch, smell, balance, and movement; all of which may be affected by the condition of the learner (needs, interests, growth, attitude, emotional state, desire at the moment of perception, strength of the stimuli, and likelihood of occurrence).

Perceptual space is geometric, so mathematical knowledge originates from contact with objects which constitute the environment. Perception enables children to comprehend spatial relationships, understand objects' movements, and coordinate their own movements with those of objects. Children who use their perceptual powers act among things and not only on things to discriminate and conceptualize by image and thought.

Although mathematical thought results from experience, experience may be defined in two ways. Interaction with objects to conceptualize is physical experience. On the other hand, logico-mathematical experience is independent of direct physical application as knowledge is not acquired from physical properties but by actions. These actions are internalized symbolic operations. In other words, logic and mathematics develop beyond a level for physical experience to become irrelevant (Piaget 1972, pp. 50-1). Children who apply logico-mathematical experience are not limited by physical properties as logic and mathematics overtake physical experience to enable higher order concepts to be formed.

As with concepts, logical thinking cannot be taught. Many young children often have as great a subtlety in their deductive powers as they will in later life. Logical thinking is developed by the extent that experience requires children to apply their mental powers. In fact, as Piaget (1973) explains, action and logico-mathematical experience do not hinder later development of deductive thought. They are a necessary preparation for it as intellectual operations stem from action.

As a result, young children vary in their degree of mathematical development. They will apply logico-mathematical experience in some instances, but in others will be at a level of physical experience. Children who depend on physical experience will be content to rely on repetition and generalization only. Returning to the example with blocks to illustrate this point, by constantly playing with blocks of different sizes a child should become aware that a block is able to be fitted on top of another block without falling off because the faces are flat. This leads to other blocks (irrespective of size) being added until a tower of four or five blocks is constructed before it falls down. A child could repeat the activity but remain content for the tower to collapse. Although he has learned a property of blocks, and used that property to erect a tower, he has not rationalized how to keep the tower stable. He has assimilated (evidence) a new concept but not modified his schema to accommodate (belief) the experience.

Another child who applies logico-mathematical experience to the activity will solve the problem. He will reason that the largest block must be put at the base with the succeeding blocks seriated by size if the tower is not to fall. He has developed beyond the physical property of the blocks to coordinate action and logico-mathematical experience to reach a solution. When a child applies logico-mathematical experience to an activity he is thinking operationally. He is extending his thought to acquire knowledge, and in the process is conceptualizing for relational understanding.

Relational understanding was described by Skemp (1976) as not only knowing what to do but why as it includes knowledge of underlying mathematical relationships and properties. It is more adaptable and more intrinsically interesting as it is less dependent on outside incentives. Instrumental understanding is when pupils and teachers think that they understand something if they are able to obtain correct answers to a given category of questions without necessarily knowing why the method works. It does not easily adapt to new requirements, and memorizing a large number of unrelated rules eventually becomes an impossible burden.

Byers and Herscovics (1977) extend Skemp's model by suggesting two further categories of understanding — intuitive understanding and formal understanding. They refer to intuitive understanding as the ability to deduce specific rules or procedures from more general mathematical relationships, and quote Bruner (1960, p.10) as their source for this definition when he states that intuition implies the act of grasping the meaning, significance, or structure of a problem without specific reliance on analysis. Byers and Herscovics question whether intuition should or could be taught in schools, and frequently refer to 'intuitive thinking'.

Backhouse (1978) refutes this interpretation as a confusion between thought and understanding particularly when intuitive understanding is specified as 'the ability to solve a problem without prior analysis of the problem'. Backhouse is correct as Danzig (1930 pp. 247-8) describes intuition as a compelling insight that enables mathematical progression without the need for logical deduction. Intuition is a 'sixth sense' that originates from innate ability to provide a correct answer to a problem. As such, it does not provide relational understanding. The individual cannot describe how he reached his conclusion. Neither is conceptualization involved as the process cannot be traced back to a starting point or assimilated into a schema. Moreover, is it possible to define a child's answer to a problem as intuition when it may have been an inspired guess? Intuition cannot be classed as understanding in mathematics as it must either return to conceptualization to acquire relational understanding or be fitted to rules to provide instrumental understanding. Thus, it is a fallacy to assume that intuition should or could be taught. Innate ability cannot be taught.

Backhouse *(op. cit.)* also criticizes Byers and Herscovics when they describe formal understanding as the ability to connect symbols and notation with relevant mathematical ideas, and combine these ideas into chains of logical reasoning. According to Byers and Herscovics, formal deduction differs from relational and instrumental understanding as these categories focus on relationships and rules respectively whereas understanding form focusses on representation and deductive reasoning. 'Form is a way of representing a concept and it is the constituent parts that should be stressed as against the more obvious spatial arrangements on paper', Backhouse argues when contending that Byers and Herscovics are concerned with rules and not concepts in their definitions of relational and instrumental understanding. Again, Backhouse is correct as the definition of formal learning by Byers and Herscovics is rote learning whereby manipulations of symbols are memorized. This is what many children do when they carry out 'long multiplication'. They have been taught to 'add a nought on the end' and this is done automatically. The notation columns are kept straight, and the correct answer is obtained. The children abide by the prescribed form, but no indication is given of whether they understand place value. They merely practise instrumental understanding to secure an answer by manipulation of symbols.

Symbols may allow the replacement of originals but the manner in which replacements are rationalized by logico-mathematical experience specifies the level of conceptualization, and the degree of thought. Consequently, children should be given opportunities to physically experience situations and derive relational understanding before being required to apply symbols. Only when conceptualization has been acquired can objects be replaced by symbols, and children understand what they are doing when manipulating form. For example, children need many experiences of grouping in 'tens' with straws, match sticks, counters, etc. before being able to appreciate place value. Likewise, experience with objects is necessary to acquire the 'numberness of number' but, once this is acquired, the objects may be replaced by numerals.

Reference to symbols emphasizes an important aspect of children's acquisition of mathematics. Words are the first mathematical symbols encountered and learned by children. Words interpret and communicate the first conceptualized spatial relationships. In number, although the 'oneness of one', 'twoness of two', etc. may be conceptualized, the information must be communicated by symbols (words) e.g. 'one', 'two', etc. before relational understanding can be ascertained.

Children's vocabulary development should proceed alongside physical and logico-mathematical experiences. Initially, names may not be of objects but the noises associated with them, e.g. puff-puff, tick-tick, quack-quack, etc., until a level of understanding is reached to discriminate between objects. Children become aware of properties which interest them, and other properties to which their attention is drawn — food is sweet or not sweet, the table is rough or smooth, a ball will roll while a box does not move, teddy is big but pussy is small, etc. Children's cognitive development depends upon the progressive classification of experiences, assisted by association with an adult or another child to interpret experience into language. Language development implies a deliberate attempt firstly to improve comprehension by facilitating the rules which determine the structure of language and, secondly, facilitating speech through the organization and realization of this knowledge of structure. Mathematical development, on the other hand, implies a deliberate attempt firstly to improve comprehension of the environment by facilitating the acquisition of concepts which determine the structure of mathematics and, secondly, through the acquisition of these concepts facilitating relational understanding through the organization and realization that the concepts provide.

Formal understanding, as defined by Byers and Herscovics *(op. cit.)*, does not provide means for children to abstract and form concepts. Their expression 'chains of logical reasoning' and insistence on rule learning are features associated with stimulus-response learning, and derive from Gagne's model of chain learning. Stimulus-response learning is instrumental learning that, according to Gagne (1977 pp.82-95), has two advantages: 1. it emphasizes the precise skilled nature of the responses involved, and 2. it implies that the learned connection is instrumental in satisfying some motive. Chaining is connecting a set of individual S — Rs in sequence with the correct links from start to finish. The individual motor chains that are learned become the components of more complex, purposeful activities called motor skills, and are later combined into organized motor performances 'which learning and continued practice invest with characteristics of smoothness and timing'.

Contrary to the prior explanations of conceptual and language development, Gagne demonstrates chain learning by verbal association through naming, and selects a child developing awareness of a tetrahedron as an example. A child is *told* while being shown a three dimensional object, 'This shape is called a tetrahedron'. The next time the child sees the particular object, and if conditions are suitable, he will be able to name it as a tetrahedron but, Gagne adds, other conditions are important. The child may not discriminate the object as a stimulus, and he may not have learned to say its name. The act of naming a tetrahedron therefore seems to be a chain of at least two links. The first link is an observing response, an S — R that connects the appearance of the object with responses involved in observing the triangular character of its sides, and at the same time distinguishes it from other three-dimensional objects of roughly the same colour and size. The second link is the S — R connection that enables a child to stimulate himself to say 'tetrahedron' as a voluntary response. With the small 's' standing for the internal representation of the object resulting from its observation, Gagne shows the act of naming by the following chain:

S ——————▶R   ∿   s ——————▶R
       object   observing   tetrahedron   'tetrahedron'

Gagne does not specify how the child internalizes to acquire representation. The child is told that the object is a tetrahedron and, depending upon the stimulus that the object creates, recalls the associated name by memory.

Being given words does not ensure that children have derived relational understanding. Abstraction must take place before this occurs. Words may convey meaning, but meaning is not understanding. This differentiates between a child who in mathematics uses language knowledgeably and a child who uses words without understanding, and is illustrated by Choat and De'Ath (1976) with an incident concerning a seven and a half year old boy. When asked to explain the definition of a half, the boy was bewildered. He was aware intuitively of a half, had done sums with halves, and possessed an adequate vocabulary to express himself, but could not explain what he meant by a half. He had been given, or had learned, the necessary vocabulary to describe a half (one over two is a half), but had not rationalized understanding.

Although Byers and Herscovics refer to 'meaningful manipulation', this does not ensure relational understanding. Teachers often remark that learning should be meaningful and distinguish between meaningful learning and rote learning. Even researchers make a distinction such as when Riedesel and Burns (1973) report that the results of studies between meaningful and mechanical learning suggest that (a) rote learning and meaning produce about the same results when immediate computational ability is used as a criterion; (b) when retention is used as a criterion, the meaning method is superior to the rote-rule method; (c) greater transfer is facilitated by the meaning method; and (d) the meaning method produces greater understanding of mathematical principles and comprehension of complex analysis.

Based on the work of Ausubel, an American psychologist, Rae and McPhillimy (1976, pp.47-63) explain that meaningful learning takes place when the learner relates new knowledge to existing knowledge that consists of previously learned theories, principles, concepts, etc. when he gives examples, answers questions by using the information, or restates the main ideas in his own words. When presenting material for meaningful learning, Rae and McPhillimy state that a teacher should ensure that existing cognitive structures are clear and stable, while similarities and differences between the new idea and the established idea should be pointed out, and the child might be given an opportunity to overlearn the material that is to be retained. How can children overlearn what is to be retained? Many adults 'overlearned' the tables of multiplication when at school by constantly chanting them, but how many remember the tables now?

Claiming that meaningful learning is more effective than rote learning as it is easier to learn, better remembered, and more transferable, Rae and McPhillimy illustrate the superiority of meaningful learning by quoting evidence from studies. In one study, children were *taught* subtraction by the decomposition method which is described, 'if we subtract 26 from 82, ten is 'borrowed' from the 80 reducing it to 70 and increasing the 2 to 12'.

$$\begin{array}{cc} {}^{7}\cancel{8} \ {}^{1}2 \\ 2 \quad 6 \\ \hline 5 \quad 6 \end{array}$$

Half of the children were taught 'borrowing' meaningfully — teachers emphasized how the procedure worked and why it gave correct results — and the other half were taught 'borrowing' as a mechanical process. The results indicated that learning and retention were superior for the children taught meaningfully, and they retained their advantage when three digit numbers were introduced.

Although these children retained their advantage by reaching a correct answer to the sum, they had acquired instrumental understanding only. The means employed to carry out the process gave no opportunity to acquire relational understanding. The word 'borrow' enables a manipulation of symbols to arrive at an answer and acquiesces with formal understanding as interpreted by Byers and Herscovics. Children do not apply the principles of place value when they 'borrow' an equivalent amount from one column to another column. In fact, they are not 'borrowing' at all but making a compensatory adjustment in the value of the quantity.

Contrary to Rae and McPhillimy, meaningful learning is a sophisticated form of rote learning. This raises the question of whether meaningful rote learning is possible as opposed to rote learning. Rote learning is unconnected learning and memorizing facts to be reproduced on demand. These facts are applied only in situations in which they were learned. Meaningful rote learning occurs when, although devoid of relational understanding, realization of facts emerges as the result of continual rote practice. The way some children apply the tables of multiplication is an example. Children are practised constantly in the tables until they realize what the tables mean. When situations arise that require the use of tables, i.e. area, the cost of a number of items, etc., the children have sufficient meaning to know that they can provide a correct answer by using tables, but understanding how the answer is reached remains a mystery. A stage is reached when rules associated with the tables are at their limit and children cannot progress further. Nevertheless, some educationalists contend that meaningful rote learning places children in a position to be able to understand at a later date, but such an argument is false. To acquire understanding, children will need to revert to rationalization of lower order concepts before being able to apply operations that require relational understanding in a higher order.

Skemp's original categories of understanding are not affected by this exposition, but further levels of understanding appear to exist. In the higher level of relational understanding, a child conceptualizes to understand through logico-mathematical experience, and in the lower level he conceptualizes through physical experience. Meaningful learning, and rote learning, are within instrumental understanding, but these two levels may merge together to provide meaningful rote learning. Intuition is not classified as understanding as it reverts either to relational understanding for conceptualization or to instrumental understanding to be fitted to rules. Diagrammatically, the levels are:

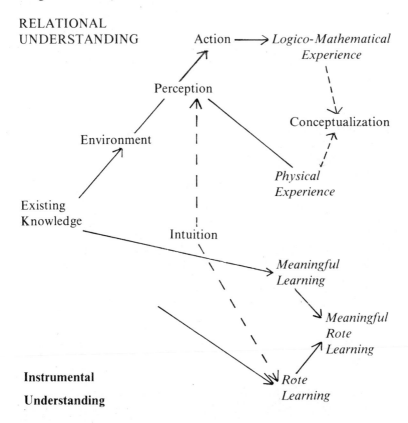

RELATIONAL
UNDERSTANDING

Action ⟶ *Logico-Mathematical Experience*

Perception

Environment

Conceptualization

Existing
Knowledge

Physical Experience

Intuition

Meaningful Learning

Meaningful Rote Learning

Instrumental

Understanding

Rote Learning

A teacher should specify the level of understanding she is defining when assessing a child for mathematical competence. To return to the classroom incidents of building a tower. Each example could apply to a different child, and each child's teacher claim that he now understands the principles of construction by discrimination of shape and size. But how many of the children have acquired relational understanding, and at what level is the understanding?

Understanding in mathematics relies on the teaching to which children are exposed; Jane being a typical example. Unfortunately, some teachers are prepared to teach without bothering about relational understanding, and, if the aspect is to be investigated with validity, teaching techniques must be evaluated also. Undoubtedly, such would involve evaluating which methods and organizations are appropriate to different levels of development and stages of mathematical progression, how progress to further development is determined, whether the organization allows for association with those children who need it, and whether pupils' outcomes match those of the teacher's expectations.

REFERENCES

BACKHOUSE, J.K. (1978). 'Understanding School Mathematics — A Comment', *Mathematics Teach,* **82,** pp.39-41.

BRUNER, J.S. (1960). *The Process of Education.* Cambridge, USA: Harvard University Press.

BYERS, V. and HERSCOVICS, N. (1977). 'Understanding School Mathematics', *Mathematics Teaching,* **81,** pp. 24-7.

CHOAT, E. and De'ATH, S. 'Epa → Spa →?' *Association of Educational Psychologists Journal,* **4,** 1, 30-4.

DANZIG, T. (1930) *Number: The Language of Science.* London: Allen & Unwin.

GAGNE, R.M. (1977) *The Conditions of Learning* (Third Edition), New York: Holt, Rinehart & Winston.

PIAGET, J. (1972) *Psychology and Epistemology.* Harmondsworth: Penguin.

PIAGET, J. (1973). 'Comments on Mathematical Education', In HOWSON, A.G. (Ed) *Developments in Mathematical Education.* London: Cambridge University Press.

RAE, G. and McPHILLIMY, W.N. (1976). *Learning in the Primary School* London: Hodder & Stoughton.

RIEDESEL, C.A. and BURNS, P.C. (1973). 'Research on the Teaching of Elementary-School Mathematics'. In: TRAVERS, R.M.W. (Ed) *Second Handbook of Research on Teaching,* Chicago: Rand McNally.

SKEMP, R.R. (1971). *The Psychology of Learning Mathematics* Harmondsworth: Pelican.

SKEMP, R.R. (1976) 'Relational Understanding and Instrumental Understanding', *Mathematics Teaching,* **77,** pp.20-6.

Chapter 4
Interlude with Jane

I met Jane and her mother during the Christmas holidays. Jane by then had reached her fifth birthday. Her first reaction was to say that she could count to a hundred, and proceeded to do so. She counted through to nineteen correctly, missed out the twenties completely, went from thirty through to forty, mumbled some incomprehensible words, and then proudly announced, 'One hundred'.

Next day, an excited Jane brought her latest mathematics book for me to look at. This was revealing. The first page showed practice of the numerals — 1, 2, 3, 4 and 5, and the next page, written by Jane, consisted of eight examples which began with

● + ●● = ●●●   and ended with   ● ● + ● ● = ●●
1 + 2 = 3

● + ●● = ●●●   and ended with   ●   ●   ●●
1 + 2 = 3   3 + 3 = 6

These sums, with some that totalled 'ten', went on for five pages, and were all correct. Four pages of examples without the dots followed. The remaining ten pages comprised addition with vertical addends, and 'ten' was still included, i.e.

$$\begin{array}{ccc} 2+ & 5+ & 4+ \\ \underline{8} & \underline{4} & \underline{3} \\ 10 & 9 & 7 \end{array}$$

Jane's only flaw was to reverse the numeral seven on some occasions. Discounting the introduction of 'ten' without relevance to place value, the progression thought suitable for Jane by her teacher was predictable but, in view of her previous performance, how had she managed to answer the sums correctly? Her mother gave the explanation. 'She counts blocks. If it's four plus three, she puts out four blocks and three blocks, and counts them'.

Jane had not been doing addition as was suggested in her book but union of sets, and finding the total number of elements by counting as in the diagram.

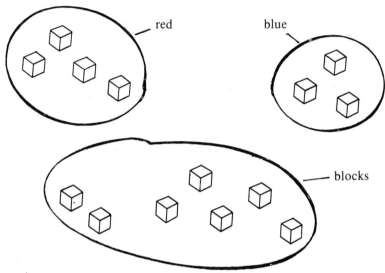

Jane was working with objects. Having combined the set of 'red' and the set of 'blue' into a set of blocks, she proceeded to count. Her mathematical activity was to practise counting; the identification between elements of a set by certain verbalizations (Choat 1978). The incident was typical of a child being fitted to mathematics. Jane needed activities to develop her experiences of the 'numberness of number'. Her book gave the impression that she was doing addition of number but this was incorrect. As Jane was operating on sets, the activities should have been recorded by visual representation.

Counting and addition are separate mathematical operations. When each element in a set is established as a unit, the appropriate verbalization by number name — one . . . two . . . three . . . four . . . five . . . etc. — is accredited to each element; the last name being the total. The counted value (natural number) is recorded by matching the appropriate symbol — 1, 2, 3, 4, 5, etc. Memory is relied upon to match the specific symbol (numeral) to the total which has been counted, i.e. 5 to 'five'. The operation of addition, on the other hand, is an abstraction and dispenses with physical objects. A child, when asked the total of 'four' and 'three' is able to answer 'seven'. When recording addition, i.e. $4 + 3 = 7$, the child must again memorize which symbols represent which numbers.

Jane visited me a week later. On this occasion the one-to-one correspondence check which she had attempted previously was replicated. Her approach was different this time. When the pencils and pennies were displayed, she carefully counted them in turn, and proclaimed the same number of each. When the pennies were readjusted into a lengthened line she maintained equivalence between the items, but when the pennies were put into a pile she changed her opinion and declared that there were more pencils.

Jane had developed in 'numberness' compared to her attempt some five months earlier, but not to the extent that she should be 'doing addition'. She had acquired the ability to count early numbers but her teacher was using this proficiency to give the impression that Jane was capable of the operation of addition. In fact, Jane had by-passed many experiences that would assist her acquisition of 'numberness of number'. It appeared that in her early number development Jane had not acquired: negative relations; mapping by one-to-one correspondence; the symbols to define more than, fewer than, and the same as; seriation; ordinal sequence; combining by pictograms; combining by sets; bilateral symmetry; patterns by translational symmetry; patterns for numbers to five; mapping to two, three, four and five; patterns for numbers from six to nine; mapping to six; seven, eight, and nine; using the number line to combine sets; and ordered pairs. Activities relating to zero were disregarded also.

What are the consequences of these episodes with Jane? A 'back to basics' advocate visiting Jane's class, and looking at her book, would be highly delighted with this five year olds' achievements. The school would be following the correct approach and teaching children some 'mathematics'. But this is far from the truth. Jane's mathematical development is woefully lacking. She has large gaps in her numerical development, and the early experiences that involve the exploration of space and shape have been ignored. Jane illustrates how a child can be manipulated to indicate that she is competent in addition. Her example shows that, unless a means of assessment which looks beneath the surface is employed, those who are unaware of the intricacies can be easily fooled.

REFERENCES

CHOAT, E. (1978). 'Matching, Corresponding and Counting', *Association of Educational Psychologists Journal,* **4,** 6, 32-5.

Chapter 5

The Role, Responsibilities and Expectations of Teachers

Human beings never stop learning. From early childhood to old age, there is always something new to learn. Much learning takes place in the activities of life, but society decided to establish schools in which it would formally educate its young. Within schools, teachers are appointed to carry out the task.

Authority is bestowed on teachers to fulfil their function in the manner which they think appropriate. Society maintains watchdogs in the guise of the Department of Education and Science, local education authorities, and governors, but the powers of these bodies are not usually called upon unless teachers offend society in some way. Obviously, society has views on what it expects from teachers. Most of the impressions are based on individuals' experiences during their own schooling, and scarcely alter. Although changing demands of society change what is expected from schools, until recently society had done little since the Education Act, 1944, to impose demands on schools. Teachers, by divorcing themselves from society, did not help the situation. Once entrusted with authority, they used it to instil their own ideas. It is now realized that the education of children is a cooperative effort between parents, society and schools.

To retain their autonomy in the face of pressure from society, teachers must take stock and examine their role, expectations and responsibilities, particularly in the teaching of mathematics. In fairness, it must be said that many primary school teachers are aware of their responsibility and wish to improve their teaching, but other teachers, suffering from their own insecurity in mathematics, have failed to come to grips with their mathematics teaching, and a minority have not given sufficient thought to their role. If teachers are to be successful they must believe in the methods they use, but this does not mean that they should never modify their thinking in the light of experience or change their ways of working (Goddard 1974 pp. 65-6). There is a need to constantly re-examine practices, and to sift and take account of new evidence and new materials. Nevertheless, Goddard admits, the role of the teacher is difficult to define, and in the last resort each teacher will work in her own way, taking into account the children for whom she is responsible, the space at her disposal, her own special interests and strengths, and the other adults who are or who may be available to help. Increasingly, teachers find that answers to problems are resolved through consultation with colleagues. One teacher may try out a certain teaching technique and then meet with her colleagues to discuss the outcome of the experiment. Teachers meet in workshops and teachers' centres with the similar purpose of examining current practices and the theories behind them.

Roles are norms which apply to categories of persons, while norms are prescriptions for behaviour. The role of a teacher is the function expected of her and, according to Blyth (1965 pp.168-72) may be classified as what a teacher does (role-performance), what a teacher is expected to do (role-expectation), what is involved in the discharge of a particular role (role-set), and the range of different roles which are involved in a particular teacher's task (role-complex). Within her role-set, a teacher may encounter role-conflict for she is expected to be an instructor for imparting knowledge and moral training, a socializer in that she is an auxiliary to parents, and value-bearer by upholding the mores and folkways of society. Therefore, a teacher has a dual responsibility (a) an authority whose task is to initiate the young into what is regarded as worthwhile in itself, and (b) an agent of selection for the emphasis which she puts on learning and socialization will affect children's outlook towards education and their eventual jobs. From the ascribed roles, a teacher attains an achieved role, within which she assumes two impressions — what she regards as her responsibilities (role-conception), and what she regards as her expectations from pupils (role-outcome).

These specifications allow a primary school teacher's role in mathematics teaching to be made more explicit. Her role-performance is her approach to the teaching of the subject. Ultimately, this performance will be judged on what children have learned. She may elect to teach formally or by new approaches, differentiate the subject or integrate it with other subjects, teach children as a class, in groups or individually, use the blackboard, structural apparatus or the environment, prepare work-cards, use text books or allow children to follow work books, rely on instrumental or relational understanding, etc. Whatever the organization, methods and content, the evaluation is whether curriculum objectives have been achieved.

This implies that role-expectation in mathematics teaching is to teach children some mathematics and, this is surrounded with controversy. Mathematics is found everywhere and in almost everything, but the failure by some teachers to recognize these facts leads to diminished expectations. Competent mathematics teaching is not possible unless teachers are aware of the mathematics which can be extracted from various learning situations. To be able to do this teachers must develop mathematical expertise and become mathematically conscious by involving themselves in the study of mathematics. This does not mean that primary school teachers should become mathematicians to the exclusion of everything else, but that they should consider the subject more than they have in the past.

This contention will be treated with scorn by some teachers. Mathematics sends them into a state of evasion. They happily discuss why language and reading are essential for primary school children, and outline what they are doing, but a reaction sets in as soon as mathematics is mentioned. These comments are not intended to be disparaging. The vast majority of teachers wish to improve their mathematics teaching. They would like to know more about mathematics, and come to terms with the subject. Their inadequacies date back to how they were taught, leaving school with an insufficient grounding in the subject owing to poor teaching, boredom or rejection.

Many primary school teachers go the wrong way about improving their mathematics teaching. They rely too much on what other people tell them. They will become better mathematical educators only by unravelling the joys of mathematics for themselves, with the assistance of others. Mathematics schemes which depend on the use of work books, or have rigid instructions have become popular in some schools, and are indications of insecurity. Irrespective of whether a scheme is sound or otherwise, some teachers have latched on to it as they are given an easy page by page continuation. Untold harm is being done to children who are subjected to this practice as the teachers often do not know what the children are doing. These teachers cannot claim to be teaching mathematics. Only when teachers can competently cater for individual progression in children, according to levels of development and pace of learning, will they fulfil role-expectation in mathematics teaching.

A teacher's role-performance and role-expectation will affect her role-set. If incompetent, she is not providing opportunities for knowledge to be acquired in mathematics, but the frustrations which a teacher may encounter in the execution of her teaching are as equally disturbing. A teacher who is ambitious to teach mathematics so that children will become interested in it may be handicapped by a lack of time allocated to the subject, insufficient materials at her disposal, an apathy towards the subject by her Head Teacher and colleagues, a compulsion to teach particular mathematical notions in specified ways, a restriction on the text or work books which she is allowed to use, a lack of finance allocated to the subject in the school, an insistence on having to teach by formal methods, confined space within the school and classroom, an obsession by her superiors for children to be constantly practised in the operations on number, the weird interpretation that two forms of mathematics exist — 'old' and 'new' mathematics, etc.

Implications relating to role-set are contained in a report by Ward (1979, pp.18-32, 51-7). In this Schools Council research project on primary mathematics, Ward maintains that a single worry stood out from the rest — neglect of the basic processes. Many teachers expressed concern that some children were not getting enough practice and revision in the fundamental skills of computation. This concentration on basic computation showed clearly in the teachers' rating of importance of mathematical topics. All the questions at the top of the rating list were concerned with operations on number, the understanding of notation and place value. The attitude was reflected in the text books found in classrooms for a high percentage of them were 'old favourites' which gave many examples in the 'four rules'. Perhaps, Ward adds, that a swing back to the basics is inevitable as swings of fashion exist in all subjects at all levels of education, but he diplomatically states, 'Perhaps in order to gain a platform some innovators find it necessary to over-state their case, to over-sell their wares'. With so many new topics introduced into primary mathematics in recent years, teachers often found it difficult to grasp the overall framework of primary mathematics, and to see the lines of progression that the various parts of the subject ought logically to follow. Related to this feeling was that teachers had tried to introduce too much too soon to children. Another concern was the amount of time which can be devoted to mathematics — both the children's time and the teacher's. Some teachers were disturbed about practical work and wondered if activities did link up with the relevant mathematical ideas in children's minds. Perhaps, Ward suggests, the slogan of the Nuffield Mathematics Project 'I do, I understand' is sometimes misunderstood. 'Do some teachers think that merely by *doing* an activity a child will understand — by the very act of going around the edge of the playground with a measuring tape will the child somehow be given a concept of distance and perimeter?' he asks. Mathematical activities are justified, not by themselves, but by what happens immediately afterwards. At that point the mathematical implications need to be drawn out, either by leading questions from the teacher, from a workcard or by children discussing things among themselves. Children must do things, and teachers need to plan and think carefully about the activities that will be most profitable to cram a crowded curriculum into a short school day.

Unquestionably, Ward remarks, mathematics now demands much more from the teacher — much more time and skill in preparing, organizing and recording, and much more understanding of mathematical concepts. Understanding, he maintains, is the key word for teachers and pupils. When asked to state the strong points of today's primary mathematics, almost half the teachers put understanding first. Because the activities and problems given to children were linked to their own experiences, teachers saw this as helping pupils to understand what mathematics is all about. The teachers were aware that individual work brought problems of its own but, when children worked individually, their rate of progress was not restricted. Bright children could be stretched and the slow-learners catered for, although without some form of prodding the pace of individual work could become leisurely.

Children who were poor readers was another aspect which Ward found affected teachers' role-set. In large classes with each child working at his own pace, it was sometimes easy for a boy or a girl to 'get stuck' or pick up the wrong idea from a workcard without the teacher being aware immediately of this. The problem of keeping efficient profiles of individual progress was also a matter of concern; in effect this being part of what may be thought of as classroom management.

In her teaching of mathematics, the primary school teacher may encounter role-conflict in her role-set. Apart from the instances which many affect her task of presenting opportunities for the acquisition of mathematics, she is faced with other circumstances which may detract from her role as socializer and value-bearer. Such issues as mentioned by Ward of children with poor reading abilities and large classes inhibit a teacher in the execution of her role. Even more disturbing is the teacher who sets out with good intentions but becomes disillusioned owing to the conditions which she encounters.

In mathematics, as well as any other subject, much socializing and bearing of values take place. Children must learn to share equipment, cooperate in learning situations, observe rules about how to behave towards other children, display attitudes and sentiments towards the teacher, etc. To accomplish this a teacher must provide a secure and relaxed environment in which respect for persons is an underlying principle. This involves establishing a firm and clear structure within which activities and interaction may occur. It is the teacher's job to provide the rules and the discipline which she regards as essential for the children's needs to be satisfied and to enable them to learn to socialize and attain autonomy (Sharp and Green 1975 p.91).

A teacher's view of her role is critical to implementation of her role-set. The question is dealt with by Sharp and Green (*ibid*, pp. 68-113) who analyse three teachers' impressions of their role in a 'progressive' primary school. One teacher, Mrs Carpenter, viewed most of her children as 'thick and those who are't thick are disturbed'. She spoke guardedly about many of the households having problems such as absent fathers, debts, eviction orders, and the disconnection of electric power. Given this teacher's attitude, it is not surprising that she considered the school's aim as being to compensate children for their underprivileged home backgrounds. She saw the children as not stable enough to be able to respond to the teaching of skills in mathematics, and entered into a serious dispute with the deputy head who favoured a structured approach with a more rigid set of aims in the form of a publicly available programme of work. Mrs Carpenter rejected the idea of a pre-planned set of intellectual pursuits in favour of a curriculum orientated to the interests of each child. She felt that she was a successful teacher, organizing her classroom on informal lines, keeping the children happy and eager to attend school, and having as good an academic attainment record as other more formal teachers.

The second teacher, Mrs Lyons, saw her pupils as the products of largely unstable and uncultured backgrounds with parents who were irresponsible, incompetent, illiterate, 'clueless', disinterested in and unappreciative of education and who, as a result, failed to prepare their children for school. She maintained that the teacher's task was not socialization but re-socialization, or attempting to compensate for the errors or deficiences of upbringing which affect a child's ability to be educated. Mrs Lyon regarded herself as a child-centred teacher, and moved to the school because of her sympathy with the headmaster's approach to education and pedagogy. Her child centredness was more an approach to the child rather than a commitment to informal methods. In this connection, she commented that even the headmaster reverted to more formal methods of teaching — organizing groups, class teaching, and being directive — when forced to take a class when teachers were absent, etc. Mrs Lyon expressed the view that play was important for socialization, but her attitude towards the activity was ambiguous. She thought dressing up 'silly', sand and water play all right but only for younger children, and frequently reminded the children that, 'You don't come to school to play all day'. Mrs Lyon spent most of her time with those children she defined as 'ready' or 'all there' and were at the stage to move on and benefit from her attention. The children tended to be older, mostly girls, who showed that they were more responsive to learning, better trained for school, and had developed manual dexterity.

The third teacher, Mrs Buchanan, instead of seeing children as deprived, maladjusted or disturbed, saw them as normal children who came from working class backgrounds. Nevertheless, she felt that they were not provided with the right kind of supportive environment. She regarded her pupils as products of an environment which they accepted as normal, and contended that teachers should recognize this and not pride themselves that they were 'doing a grand job because they're in that school and, you know, what a good thing they're doing for these children'. Yet when speaking of individual children's failures she attributed the causes to difficulties or problems in the homes. She considered the school's methods as not suitable for the type of child with whom she had to deal. Given a free hand, she would have had the children sitting at certain times of the day for reading, writing and number work. The combination of children moving around, noise, and the pupils' disinterest in any of the activities, presented Mrs Buchanan with discipline problems. She adopted a *laissez faire* attitude to new children and tended to let them find their own feet. This notion of a teacher playing a passive role in the settling-in process did not characterize her view of teaching. She recognized that a proficient teacher must organize her classroom but considered her own failure as her inability to organize adequately, and would have been grateful for help from more experienced teachers. Mrs Buchanan regarded herself as a teacher when she was interacting with a child about work; when helping with reading, writing and number work. Her plan was to introduce an activity and proceed to 'do the rounds' by moving from group to group, child to child. She felt that children should get on alone for 'unless they can work on their own, the children are in difficulties'.

These examples show that there is nothing ordinary about teaching in the primary school and, when related to mathematics, nothing ordinary about teaching mathematics to ordinary children, contrary to what many of the 'back to basics' advocates assume. Children are individuals who differ in needs, interests, growth, intelligence, ability, attitude, emotional state, etc. They are not passive objects, but beings who exert influence on a teacher, and who affect her maintenance of social order in the classroom. The contraints, Sharp and Green (*ibid*, p.116) contend, are such that role-expectation of a teacher may well be incompatible, thus creating role-conflict.

Taking into account the factors of role-conflict, teachers acquire a range of different roles in the task of teaching (role-complex), but undertake what they belive to be their intended role. The interpretation of this role is gathered from impressions gained from society, superiors, colleagues, educationalists, parents, pupils, and their own belief of their function. This becomes their ascribed role from which they assume two designations — (a) role-conception — what they believe their responsibilities to be, and, (b) role-outcome — what they regard as their expectations from pupils.

A teacher's first responsibility is to pursue the aims of the school and interpret these into classroom objectives. She has a responsibility to stimulate learning and bring it about in the most productive way. She should attempt to accrue motivation in her pupils, but this will depend on the presentation of learning experiences. She should consider whether the curriculum content is presented better by specialization or by integration, whether she has specified the correct sequences and stages of content appropriate to children's needs, and whether the children will be able to understand her teaching presentation. Within her teaching, she must take into account, and allow for, individual differences in children, the sorts of activities which will fulfil the needs of children, the different abilities, interests and backgrounds that children take to group situations, and the extent to which teacher association plays in learning.

These responsibilities are pertinent to the teaching of mathematics. A teacher must ensure that she is presenting the subject in an interesting way; that the children are captivated by the subject and do not reject it as happened so often in the past. She must decide whether continuity in mathematics learning is possible by integrating curriculum content, i.e. a project or centre of interest, or whether it is essential that mathematics be treated as a subject in its own right. Her decision will be based on how she views mathematical progression; whether she plots a pattern of mathematical development for children or whether she is content to undertake mathematics when and how it occurs in the integration. Most teachers would choose the first option for then they have the opportunity to specify what they consider appropriate for children in their varying levels of development. The adoption of this approach requires a teacher to ensure that children have acquired prior concepts before proceeding to new learning. She must then present learning in an interesting way by selecting the appropriate apparatus, work card, text book, or activity for children to be able to understand. This entails breaking-down stages of learning into sequences which are within the capabilities of children. Moreover, she should not be content to approach an area of learning in a specified and repetitive way. This is pertinent to the tables of multiplication. Children do not acquire the tables by endlessly monologuing them. There are many varied and interesting activities at a teacher's disposal for presenting tables to children. Above all, a teacher has a responsibility for ensuring that children are attaining in mathematics, and this will transpire only when children are motivated.

As each teacher associates with children and, as she studies their behaviour, she will devise her own strategies of stimulation. These, according to Troutman (1973), will evolve if she, (a) encourages children to respond to situations using their own ideas, language patterns, and vocabulary; de-emphasizing the use of formal terminology, (b) builds activities that enlist the cooperative efforts of children; allows children to discuss their mathematical understanding, (c) selects mathematical teaching aids that provide appropriate stimuli for a given learning task, (d) constructs learning experiences so that children can focus on specific learning tasks and are not confused by related learning tasks, (e) asks creative questions and allows children time for finding thoughtful answers, and (f) selects learning situations in which children can experience success.

These strategies do not apply only to mathematics. They are

relevant to almost every area of content in the curriculum. To implement them, a teacher must pay attention to another curriculum component — method. Method is often confused with organization. Whereas organization is the systematic structure that enables learning to occur, method is the means employed by a teacher whereby interaction between the learner and some other person, object, or experience takes place to bring about learning. In this sense, education, and particularly primary education, is an extension of the weaning processes of early childhood (Wall, 1969). Mathematical thought and method are basic to this in the same way as communication, reading and writing. Concepts and skills are not confined to the content of conventional mathematics any more than reading is confined to literature. Experience relevant to a child's ability and level of development brings about a closer approach to reality; a weaning from wishes and fantasy to fact and causality. Rational thought, marshalling evidence, establishing hypotheses and evaluating outcomes are all responsibilities of a teacher and she must consider them in her teaching.

Learning should be learner-centred, but what a teacher does is of great importance. What she does pervades all learning as much on the emotional level as on the intellectual level. Her responsibility to establish personal relationships with her class, and the maintenance of class behaviour are implicit within successful teaching. A situation must ensue whereby the authority of the teacher is voluntary accepted by the class.

A distinction between personal relations and personal relationships is made by Hirst and Peters (1970, pp. 93—105). Personal relations they define as whether a teacher is friendly, cruel, or kind to her pupils, and whether they like or dislike, trust or distrust, envy or admire her and so on. Personal relations are individual for a teacher is a human being as well as an occupant of a role, and, in dealing with other human beings, the teacher is bound to react differently to each child in her class. The teacher may like some children whilst she may dislike others, but reactions are not laid down by her role. The reactions are part of the emotional and motivational climate on which a teacher bases consistent forms of conduct.

Personal relationships are more structured and grow up between, or are entered into, by the people concerned, and within them is an element of reciprocity. In a developed personal relationship, people reveal things to each other to the extent that they build a common world which they share. The content does not matter so much as the aspect under which the content is viewed. This must be a response to another. A human being is subject to pleasure and pain, and other emotions and desires. Within teaching, personal relationships are the recognition by the teacher of children as individuals and vice versa. Each is recognized as a human being by the other, but most primary school children are too immature for the degree of reciprocity necessary for such relationships. Instead, Hirst and Peters *(ibid)* feel that an embryonic personal relationship, not incompatible with the teacher's role, is set up. They advocate that a teacher should not discharge her functions entirely within the code dictated by her role and by general moral principles, but should, at the same time, allow glimpses of herself as a human being and be receptive to this dimension in her pupils. Such embryonic personal relationships dispel remoteness, and convey to children that they are meeting a live human being as well as a teacher. Nevertheless, it takes experience and judgement for a teacher to behave in this way and to gauge the correct balance between what is demanded by her role, by manners, and by morality, and what is being asked from her as a human being. A teacher at the early stage of primary education would not be successful if she were impersonal in her relationships. A teacher cannot provide conditions in which young children will learn unless she behaves like a mother.

The examples of the teachers quoted previously emphasize that personal relationships in the primary school depend on the experience and values which children bring to school from their homes and neighbourhood, and those expected by the teacher. If a teacher is to influence learning, her feelings and aspirations must interact positively with the feelings and aspirations of her pupils. With positive reciprocity between the teacher and the taught, there is a describable curricular reality with the teacher contributing to the learning (Morrell, 1969). Without reciprocity, mutual emotional satisfaction cannot exist. The curriculum remains an idea in the mind of the teacher; although the teacher teaches and the children go through the motions of learning. Learning may take place for those children who have strong feelings and aspirations imported from home. They will establish a direct relationship with books and other material available despite the teacher's inability to establish a personal relationship. Other children may learn to reject school as a boring, irrelevant place. Their learning will not be part of a curriculum described as an organized, purposive association in children's learning. Indeed, Morrell claims, with negative reciprocity, curricular reality is likely to be destructive or diseducative.

The curriculum, according to Morrell, is a structure erected on a base of reciprocal personal relationships. In curriculum, teachers are concerned with human beings whose feelings and aspirations are more real and immediately important to them than the cognitive development which is the educator's stock-in-trade. Education is not an end in itself. It is a tool and product of successful living, a means of maximizing the emotional satisfactions of being alive, and an aid of coming to terms with pain, suffering and death. Morrell insists that he is not contending that learning is irrelevant, or that cognitive development is of secondary importance. On the contrary, it does matter what children learn, and cognitive development is important. It is a waste of time to fuss about what teachers think children should learn if they do not understand how to organize a system of teacher—pupil relationships to bring about learning. Cognitive development is not detached from growth towards emotional maturity. It is the tool and the product of the growth. To live is to feel. To know and to think is to acquire the ability to select responses to environmental pressures and opportunities that maximize a feeling of well-being or happiness.

Establishing a healthy classroom atmosphere depends on a teacher's respect for her pupils. This, in turn, engenders a respect for the teacher from her pupils. Within her responsibility, a teacher has a duty to cater for the needs and interests of children. Needs may vary according to the type of school, background of the children, etc., and interests may vary according to maturity, sex of the children, etc. A book could be written about the problems raised by needs and interests may vary according to maturity, sex of the children, etc. according to each child's level of development and pace of learning is a desired ideal, but according to Hirst and Peters *(op. cit.* pp.32-9) an analysis of the concept of 'need' gives little support for optimism. Indeed, they maintain, it is a child-centred way of re-stating what should be regarded as aims of education, and leaves the motivational problem untouched. An analysis of 'need' reveals that it involves conceptions of value, and not all needs are motivational in character.

Maslow (1943) alleges that need serves as a force to direct behaviour towards goals which an individual perceives as rewarding, and which reduce tension. He specifies a hierarchy of needs — physiological needs (sleep, thirst, etc.), safety needs (also freedom from anxiety and other psychological threats), love needs (acceptance from parents, teacher, and peers), esteem needs (mastery of experiences, confidence in one's ability), and need for self-actualization (creative self-expression, attempt to satisfy one's curiosity, etc.). Maslow suggests that unless a lower need is partially fulfilled, it is difficult for a higher need to be satisfied fully. Although this hierarchy of needs specifies a different status of needs, what sort of need is referred to within the content of education? Children also need to learn some early mathematics, to read, to write and to spell and, they will be unable to fill their role as citizens in society unless they acquire concepts and skills in these subjects.

Needs may be relevant in another way when they refer to teaching. Satisfaction of them may be a necessary condition of learning other things (Hirst and Peters *op. cit.*). Needs may be implicit prior to learning. Some children may be affected by emotional problems while others may have physical disabilities which should be taken into account before learning is presented to them. Other children may have psychological needs which may affect their degree of motivation.

Ambiguity surrounds interest for it can be interpreted in a valuative and psychological sense (Hirst and Peters, *op. cit.*). A teacher is concerned with a child's interest in a valuative sense as she has to watch over the child's interest, and what courses of action are likely to maximize the child's opportunities for furthering his interest. In this capacity, a teacher makes moral decisions and takes courses of action which she considers in the child's interest, but her action may not awaken response in the child. Children do not always want to do what is in their interest to do.

On the other hand, the psychological interpretation of interest has motivational relevance. If a child is interested in something he tends to pay attention to it. He is prepared to put his mind to his interest and pursue it endlessly. Such interest may not only originate in school but outside school from association with peers, from the television, from within the family, etc. But should outside interests determine the content of education? Children may have interests which are educationally undesirable or they may be content to pursue only one avenue of interest such as boys with football and girls with 'pop' stars. A child's interest could be of educational value and a way into the curriculum, but there may be many other things which he 'needs' to learn although he has not the slightest interest.

While teaching and learning processes should keep in step with children's levels of psychological development, the same applies to motivation. Children's interests may be used by a teacher to motivate children in her planned teaching. Activities may be devised in mathematics which fit in with children's interests so that eventually the mathematics becomes the passion and the interests disappear into insignificance.

Needs and interests should be distinguished from wants. Needs and interests relate to the individual, and are determined by valuative and psychological principles. Wants, on the other hand, are impositions that originate through a pre-determined auspice. A teacher, when deciding her responsibility, must clarify whether she is to pay attention to needs and interests in children or acquiese to the wants of herself and others. This resolve affects the teaching of mathematics to primary school children. The teacher may pay attention to children as individuals and attempt to provide a mathematical education which awakens in them qualities which are essential if they are to lead a full and active life, or resort to teaching the wants that others feel is the mathematics that primary school children should learn.

The teacher has a choice and how this choice is exercised depends on her inclination to either child-centred or knowledge-centred education, along with the emphasis laid down by the school. The issue complicates a teacher's role-set and, after a time, she may find her ideologies are in conflict with the task of teaching. Apart from the responsibility which a teacher has to her pupils, she has a responsibility to society. Does a teacher who has a child-centred faith abandon her ideals in face of the criticisms being levelled at mathematics teaching and resort to teaching that emphasizes operations on number? Or has she sufficient faith to believe that what she is doing is an adequate preparation for her pupils into society?

Answers to these questions, and a summation of the teacher's role and responsibilities, are given by extracts taken from teachers' accounts of how they see their role:

" 1. I must observe my children' needs, backgrounds, personalities and stages of development in order to provide the environment and the materials to help them form their intellectual and moral reasoning powers.

2. Having set the scene, the teacher's role is vital. She must point the children's enquiries, stimulate discussion, and extend their thinking. She must assess their cognitive development at every stage and provide materials to challenge each stage.

3. The teacher must establish a close relationship with the child, establish a rapport and interact in all the child's

activities by identifying problems and helping the child to solve them. In this way, adequate means of communicating his thoughts are made available to the child and he is able to store his experiences in the form of words as well as concepts."

"Although the wealth of ideas to tackle in mathematical areas alone is vast, the thought must be to select those activities which will promote a desired sequence of behaviour and gaining of experience and vocabulary through play. The teacher in these circumstances does not need "facts at her fingertips" so much as the need to know each child well enough as to be aware of their individual needs. Through observation, it was apparent that more was received from a child engaged in a 1:1 situation, and also if the teacher looked at the child while speaking to him or her — not standing behind speaking to the back of the child's head. Apart from being impolite, the child must feel a certain insensitivity to a voice which is lost, and loses the intimacy a young child needs — especially in working at a problem which he finds difficult.

Even when working with children of an older age, it is of advantage if the teacher does not preach from the blackboard and then sit back in a chair behind an awe-inspiring table (defence mechanism on the part of the teacher!). It would be of value to some teachers of older aged pupils to see the value of play in the early stages of mathematics teaching and use it. The activities could be varied, but not to the extent that their purpose is defeated.

Organization is a vitally important part of mathematics teaching. The sequences of development in any pursuit viz. measuring, mass, computation, etc. should not be dismissed lightly as they are of prime importance. In mathematics, as in all teaching, the chronological age of the child is not as important as progression of his or her understanding through various patterns of study. If one such sequence is followed it is very easy to involve many other subjects around mathematics. Often a 'topic' is chosen and every type of link with it explored. Few teachers think of the topic coming from mathematics itself and extending it out from that base.

The teacher's role in any situation is of much importance, and it is in the teaching of mathematics. An understanding adult is the key to children's orientations towards learning — an understanding of their needs, awareness of the relevant materials to meet their needs, a person who is prepared to patiently guide and sympathise with them in difficulties and stress, and who will provide the necessary vocabulary. The teacher's role is not one of intervention — this "kills" rather than aids in any way — rather she interacts. The teacher gleans as much information out of a situation by firstly taking a participant role and observing as much as possible. She then offers the child an insight into the activity with which he is involved by becoming part of the activity herself. Interaction will then lead to an extension and development be it adding the necessary vocabulary, guiding in the direction to obtain the solution to a problem, or sorting out a confusion. Not least of all, the teacher's role in mathematical learning should be to create an environment which provides security, encourages individual confidence and stimulates calm and orderliness."

There is a contrast in role-conception held by these teachers compared to those quoted by Sharp and Green *(op. cit.)*. These are motivated teachers who were prepared to examine their role-set in order to improve their teaching of mathematics. If the challenge to primary school teachers is to be met with answers assembled from evidence in classrooms, other teachers must be prepared to enhance their professional competence.

From the implementation of role-set and role-conception, a teacher's expectations from her pupils (role-outcome) will emerge, but expectations may be biased according to whether she is child-centred or knowledge-centred in her teaching. A child-centred advocate will stress self-expression in children to foster what is individual in each case, value social and emotional aims, pay attention to needs and interests, emphasize practical experiences, seek to develop creativity, and wish for children to enjoy school. The teaching climate will be open with flexible expectations. The knowledge-centred advocate will stress the promotion of a high level of academic attainment with acquisition of the basic skills in reading, writing and arithmetic, concentrate on conventional lessons, and define 'standards' for the whole class. The teaching climate will be closed with rigid expectations and, according to Froome (1970, p.123), appear as a businesslike system where everybody knows what is expected of him.

Irrespective of whether the approach is child-centred or knowledge-centred pupil-outcome centres around the stimulation offered which in turn engenders a self-fulfilling prophecy in children. Put in another way, expectations from pupils are defined as inferences which teachers make about present and future academic achievements, and general classroom behaviour of children. Irrevocably, however the situation is viewed, teachers' expectations from children revolve around how the children apply themselves to learning and study. Most teachers, whatever their objectives and whatever style they adopt, include instruction (teaching, explaining, promoting children's understanding of and interest in whatever they are learning) and controlling children (creating an orderly atmosphere in the classroom in the interests of the pupils' own freedom to learn, to choose, to live and work with others) as important parts of their job (Downey, 1977, pp.49-50). Downey remarks that pupils' roles are seen in relation to a teacher's own role-conception, and pupil behaviour is seen favourably when it lends support to the teacher's definition of her position. She states that studies have shown most teachers to select three main areas of pupil behaviour as important — obedience, industry and motivation, and politeness. Teachers are likely to stress one of these aspects as more important than the others so children have to learn not only what constitutes a general pupil role but what a particular teacher selects as her ideal pupil role.

Outcomes expected from pupils are taken to the classroom or are quickly acquired by a teacher. They may concern (a) whether norms are fixed for the whole class or whether norms relate to individuals, (b) belief in the rigidity or flexibility of children's ability and intelligence, (c) consideration of children's potential by benefiting from teaching, (d) consideration of children attaining the potential by benefiting from learning through understanding, (e) determination of the level of difficulty presented to children either as a class, group or as individuals, and (f) an attitude to whether pupils's behaviour can be changed. The extent of the expectations will be based on the teacher's considerations of productivity and anticipations based on (a) pupils' test performances, perceived ability and intelligence, past performances, comments from previous teachers, knowledge of social circumstances (home background, environment, etc.), pupils' emotional reactions, known physical disabilities, and school records, (b) association within the classroom, e.g. needs and interests, motivation, compliance with schools rules, work habits, etc., and (c) attitude to the curriculum, i.e. the esteem in which aims, objectives, organization, method, content, and evaluation are held.

Within these prerogatives are the critical issues of the accuracy of the expectations and the teacher's willingness to accept flexibility of her anticipations. Inaccurate expectations by a teacher may cause harm to children if she is unwilling to change what she has anticipated. The issue should not be clouded by excuses for failure in 'priority' schools with such terms as 'negative rebelliousness', 'a family's child-centredness', 'cultural outlook', and 'the educational disadvantage of being born the child of an unskilled worker is both financial and psychological . . .', (Choat and De'Ath, 1976). The attitude reflected by these sort of phrases is described by Goodacre (1968) when she remarks that 'teachers tend to think of pupils from lower working class areas not only as social homogeneous groups but also as being intellectually homogeneous'. Booth, Moseley and Robertson (1974) also state, 'there are far too many children who feel that no-one is really interested in what they say or do'. Perhaps terms such as 'working class' and 'disadvantaged' evoke anticipations of poor performance and set up conditions in schools and classrooms which confirm teachers' expectations.

Although questionable statistically and methodologically, a study which focussed attention on teachers' expectations of pupils was carried out by Rosenthal and Jacobson (1968). In the study, teachers were told that unusual intellectual gains would be expected from certain children (aged six to twelve years) who in fact did not possess unusually high IQs. Along with control children, these experimental children were re-tested over the next year and a half. The experimental six and seven year olds showed substantial gains in test performance when compared to the control children. When asked their opinions, the teachers described the experimental children as being happier, more curious and more interesting than the control children, and referred to the experimental children as more appealing, more affectionate, less in need of social approval, and having a better chance of success in later life. Although many of the control children made gains also, the more they gained the less favourably they were rated by the teachers.

Morrison and McIntyre (1969 p.182) make pertinent observations on the study. They state that a source of information provided from outside the classroom can be a powerful corrective to teachers' personal assessments of pupils. Secondly, without some external reference, teachers' assessments may form part of a confirmation process rather than a means to the better understanding of pupils' capabilities or difficulties. Lastly, there are no neat and specific consequences from a teacher discovering something new about her pupils.

An interesting revelation of the Rosenthal and Jacobson study was the communication of the expectations held by the teachers to the pupils. As a result, the pupils responded with higher scholastic performances. This reaction is known as the self-fulfilling prophecy and, according to Nash (1976 p.15) assumes certain propositions to be true. First, a teacher's expectations about pupils will be communicated to them. Second, the pupils will respond to this knowledge, and not to some unknown factor. Third, these processes take place without necessary conscious awareness by the people concerned. There are however possibilities of exceptions. A teacher's expectations may not be so automatically self-fulfilling as was suggested. Some pupils may resist a teacher and force changes from the original expectations. The likelihood exists also of a teacher treating a pupil differently from what he is if her initial belief is inaccurate. Thereby, self-fulfilling prophecies may affect classroom behaviour and, according to Good and Brophy (1973), could occur when a teacher expects specific behaviour and achievement from particular children, behaves differently towards different children, tells each child what behaviour and achievement she expects from him to affect his self-concept, motivation, and level of aspiration, and is consistent over time for children not to resist or change. The latter aspect encourages children with high expectations to achieve at a high level, but discourages children with low expectations so that their achievement declines.

The disturbing feature of these effects is the decline in achievement of children with low expectations. Although not conscious that they are doing so, teachers may communicate their anticipations to the children in a number of ways. Teacher characteristics are soon recognized by children and may include any of the points listed by Good and Brophy (1977 pp.386-8) — waiting less time for low achievers to answer, not staying with low achievers in failure situations, rewarding inappropriate behaviour of low achievers, praising low achievers less frequently than high achievers, not giving feedback to responses of low achievers, paying less attention to low achievers, calling on low achievers less often, differing interaction patterns with high achievers and low achievers, seating low achievers farther away, and demanding less from low achievers.

These teacher characteristics emphasize capability differences by favouring the more able children. This exaggerates and extends the initial differences which existed. Inevitably, in a mixed ability class, children themselves will be aware of their rating within the class by contrasting the work which is given them, but a teacher can accentuate differences by allowing the high achievers to dominate classroom activities, constantly seeking their answer to questions, appointing them to bear responsibility and monitorial tasks, etc. Some teachers manage to avoid these expressive expectations, and organize their classroom and teaching so that time and learning are comparable with children's needs. The contention could be raised that this is another form of expressive expectation as children with the most needs will be those who are not achieving.

Obviously, a teacher's attitude affects the motivational level of her class. Her prime concern should be to mould the class as a social unit, and for children to respect each other albeit that they differ in capability and levels of achievement. She must acknowledge also that her patterns of expectation will operate irrespective of whether the class is streamed or non-streamed. Children are not the same, and even in a streamed class there will be capability differences but a danger exists that expectations for some children will be inappropriate. Children who are cooperative with the teacher may encourage false expectations, whereas uncooperative children may instil an unpleasant impression and be given expectations which can never be fulfilled. A situation could be reached where a teacher may go out of her way to avoid uncooperative children. Expectations based on impressions tend to encourage a teacher to blame pupils in cases of failure. The teacher is alert for what she expects, and less likely to approve, or even notice, what she does not expect. Often, failure exaggerates difficulties and exacerbates problems, whereas the cause of failure is quite likely to be the teacher's teaching.

What are the expected outcomes in mathematics from children in the primary school? Teachers have a responsibility to maintain levels of expectation, and require qualities of excellence from children, but how are these qualities of excellence in mathematics obtained? There must be curriculum objectives, otherwise there would be no intended outcomes. Some people see the objectives as the acquisition of stipulated mathematical content acquired at specific ages. If this is the desired outcome, who decides the content and what is the criterion of decision? Society may list specific areas of mathematics which children should learn, but these could resolve into restricted areas of arithmetic. Alternatively, does the teacher view qualities of excellence in mathematics as a framework based on reciprocal relationships which produce intended outcomes? Thereby, is she catering for the needs and interests of her pupils and treating these as her objectives within which she feels children need to learn some mathematics? The eventual result depends on a teacher's attitude to the curriculum and the esteem in which her objectives, organization, method, content, assessment and evaluation are held. Within her appraisal, the teacher should not escape paying attention to the development of children, for them to acquire understanding, the maintenance and the furthering of the knowledge-ideal, the transmission of values, and the socialization of children in terms of expectation of society for the role of the teacher revolves around each of the aspects (Evetts, 1973, p.51).

A teacher cannot clarify her objectives until she had sound reasons psychologically for adopting them. Objectives cannot be determined before a curriculum appropriate to children's levels of development has been prepared. If the aim of mathematics teaching is to develop in children an ability to come to terms with the world in which they live, by seeing, appreciating and using the aesthetic qualities which mathematics gives to life, and using the relationships, concepts and skills of mathematics to cope with what they will encounter, objectives have to be elucidated. Objectives will be feasible only by psychological assessment with reasons resolved why the teaching should be executed in ways to achieve them. Glenn (1977, p.52) asserts that 'the logic of mathematics rarely agrees with the psychology of learning', but later adds, 'mathematics needs to be planned around the needs and interests of children'. These statements are contradictory, and the first statement is misleading. If the psychology of learning does not align with the logic of mathematics, psychological levels of development and their relationship to mathematical development are of no avail. The degree to which children aspire in mathematics depends on the psychological factors of ability, intelligence, perception, abstraction, motivation, play, etc. and how these factors relate at any given time to the notion of mathematics being learned. In other words, the psychology of learning enables fitting mathematics to children rather than children to mathematics as Glenn's statement implies.

It should not be overlooked that teaching can influence mathematical development. Children's outcomes depend on a teacher's awareness of how children acquire mathematics, factors likely to retard development, features related to progression, presentation of learning and the opportunities provided to use mathematics in other areas of curriculum content. The outcomes are still further dependent on the psychological assessment of needs combined with the motivation derived from interest. Thus, the extent of psychological assessment of outcomes determines a teacher's approach to her objectives. If she believes that purposeful association is her means she will adopt techniques that enable relational understanding to be acquired by her pupils, but, if she believes children should 'perform' the basics in arithmetic, she will resort to means that produce instrumental understanding.

The issue evolves into how society wishes its children to be educated in mathematics. Does it wish to have children who are mechanically proficient or does it wish to have children who have developed a capability to think? If the aim of the primary school curriculum is to offer experiences that will explain their world to children and develop understanding to cope sensibly with life, only one answer is possible. A teacher will secure her intended outcomes through a mathematical education which awakens in children an interest in the relevance of mathematics to life; a desire to use their ability to ask questions, intepret their actions, and communicate their experiences; a concern with the patterns and structures of their world; and a tenacity and will to further their inquiries. She will promote a teaching and learning climate that will transgress into other areas of the curriculum. Irrespective of whether it is 'traditional' or 'new' mathematics, attention has been focussed on mathematical content while insufficient consideration has been given to the equally important factors of children and how they learn. If society stipulates expectations from teachers, and teachers expect outcomes from their pupils, a new and refreshing attitude must prevail; an attitude derived from a logical deduction of the curriculum that enables mathematics to be fitted to children.

REFERENCES

BLYTH, W.A.L. (1965). *English Primary Education*. London: Routledge & Kegan Paul.

BOOTH, T., MOSELEY, D. and ROBERTSTON, J. (1974). 'Learning to Communicate', *Association of Educational Psychologists Journal,* **3,** 6, 37-53.

CHOAT, E. and De'ATH, S. (1976). 'Epa → Spa → ?', *Association of Educational Psychologists Journal,* **4,** 1, 30-4.

DOWNEY, M. (1977). *Interpersonal Judgements in Education*. London: Harper & Row.

EVETTS, J. (1973). *The Sociology of Educational Ideas*. London: Routledge & Kegan Paul.

FROOME, S. (1970). *Why Tommy Isn't Learning*. London: Tom Stacey.

GODDARD, N. (1974). *Literacy: Language – Experience Approaches*. London: Macmillan.

GOOD, T.L. and BROPHY, J.E. (1973) *Looking in Classrooms*. New York: Harper & Row.

GOOD, T.L. and BROPHY, J.E. (1977). *Educational Psychology*. New York: Holt, Rinehart & Winston.

GOODACRE, E.J. (1968). *Teachers and their Pupils' Home Backgrounds*. Windsor: NFER Publishing Company.

GLENN, J.A. (Ed.) (1977). *Teaching Primary Mathematics*. London: Harper & Row.

HIRST, P.H. and PETERS, R.S. (1970). *The Logic of Education*. London: Routledge & Kegan Paul.

MASLOW, A.H. (1943). 'A Theory of Human Motivation', *Psychological Review,* **50,** pp.370-96.

MORRELL, D. (1969, 19 December). 'Happiness is not a Meal Ticket', *The Times Educational Supplement*.

MORRISON, A. and McINTYRE, D. (1969). *Teachers and Teaching*. Harmondsworth: Penguin.

NASH, R. (1976). *Teacher Expectations and Pupil learning*. London: Routledge & Kegan Paul.

ROSENTHAL, R. and JACOBSON, L. (1968). *Pygmalion in the Classroom*. New York: Holt, Rinehart & Winston.

SHARP, R. and GREEN, A. (1975). *Education and Social Control*. London: Routledge & Kegan Paul.

TROUTMAN, A.P. (1973) 'Strategies for Teaching Elementary School Mathematics', *The Arithmetic Teacher,* **20,** 6, 425-36.

WALL, W.D. (1969, 12 September). 'The Basic Skills', *Teachers' World*.

WARD, M. (1979). *Mathematics and the ten-year-old*. London: Evans/Methuen Education.

Chapter 6
Changes in the Primary School: Their Effect on the Curriculum, and the Teaching of Mathematics

DURING the era of the elementary schools, children were ascribed to classes by achievement. Schools were all aged and catered for children from five to thirteen (later fourteen) years of age. Children were promoted according to achievement in reading, writing and arithmetic until they reached the top class — Standard One. 'High' achievers would be in Standard One at an early age and remain there until they left school, but 'low' achievers did not proceed very far up the school.

Although some local education authorities created primary and senior schools in the 1920s and 1930s, rapid change materialized after the Education Act, 1944. The Act professed education according to age, ability, and aptitude. This introduced the tripartite system of grammar, technical, and secondary schools with an examination at eleven years of age to determine the schools to which children would be allocated. As a result, streaming of children in primary schools was introduced. The origin of streaming can be attributed to the Hadow Report (1931 para. 66) which stated that, in view of the varying attainments of children, classification according to ability would lighten the task of the teacher. A triple track system of organization was recommended viz. 'A' classes for the bright children, 'B' classes for the average children, and 'C' classes for retarded children, with the belief that children of like ability would develop satisfactorily if surrounded by others of like potential, but segregation began in the Infants' School for many children.

Streaming became the means of selecting children in the early years of the primary school for their choice of secondary school. The segregation enabled the 'A' class to be coached in preparation for the eleven-plus examination, and possible entry to a selective school. The tripartite system has been removed by many LEAs in favour of comprehensive schools, so the eleven-plus examination has tended to disappear and with it the practice of streaming in primary schools. Instead, non-streaming, grouping children in classes of mixed ability, has become the common practice.

The eleven-plus dictated what was taught, and the organization, in primary schools. Its removal and the adoption of mixed ability grouping accompanied changes in mathematical content. Thus, a completely different ethos prevailed. Children are aware of the 'A', 'B', or 'C' tags, and adjust their personality and goals accordingly. The 'A' children adopt an elitist attitude and consider themselves superior to lower streams. The 'C' children become resigned to their lot, and realize that they have little hope of academic achievement. This results in apathy and rejection which, in turn, encourages despair, failure and resentment and the creation of gangs. Mixed ability grouping attempts to remove social discriminations, and allows children to be recognized as individuals. Non-categorization stimulates an environment whereby children may achieve according to their respective abilities.

Mixed ability teaching transforms a school. Class teaching, a common feature of streaming, diminishes and is replaced by individual and group teaching. This encourages child centredness; a situation which is inevitable with wide differences in ability and attainment of the children who form a class. This may present problems with the teaching of mathematics. For example, in a fourth year junior school class, some of the children may be capable of undertaking work with elementary algebra, coordinates and vectors, probability, etc. while some other children are only at the stage of attempting to achieve in the operations of number. The teacher must therefore systematize how her teaching is to be organized. She must prepare for each child. This she may do by grouping together those children who have reached a similar stage in their development while making provisions for those children who will continue with individual work. The management of such a system is not as difficult as some teachers imagine. The teacher must first diagnose each child's level of mathematical development. When this has been done, she must decide the appropriate paths of development for each child, and ensure that foundation concepts have been acquired before proceeding to higher order concepts. Such an analysis dismisses a stipulated mathematics scheme for primary school children. The teacher should have a basic framework of mathematics in her own mind, otherwise she is unable to assess children's mathematical development and associate profitably in learning situations, but she should not force a fixed pattern of progression on children. Her task is to provide a climate that will encourage activities and experience relevant to each child's level of development. Class lessons should not be dismissed entirely as occasions arise when they are beneficial. For instance, if something concerning wallpaper patterns arises in the course of the children's work, the teacher might take the opportunity to present translational symmetry to the class. After the initial introduction and preliminary work, the children may diversify in their activities. Some children could explore aspects relating to transformations, while children who were still concerned with the tables of multiplication could use translational patterns to aid understanding of the tables.

The individuality of mixed ability teaching inevitably encourages a teacher to adopt flexibility in her teaching, and in the associated forms of organization. The traditional primary school classroom consists of rows of desks with the class a closed community and taught by its own teacher for every lessons. At the other extreme is an open school which has no defined classes; the children and teachers share the whole area of the school. If left completely unstructured, such schools, known as *open plan schools,* could give an aimless appearance with children wandering at will from one place to another. This is not the case as young children need the security of a person and a place where they belong. This area is known as the home base and children report there for registration and other administrative details. In addition, there are other resource areas to use as a library, and for workshops, tape recording, viewing television, listening to music, etc. To cope with this, school furniture underwent transformation to permit layouts to be modified quickly to meet changing requirements. In height and shape, the furniture was dimensionally coordinated so that tables and work-tops could be assembled and re-assembled, but be light enough to be removed by children, and strong enough to withstand increased strain.

Apart from recently built schools being constructed as open plan, some older schools were converted to be more conducive to this way of working. Doorways, corridors, archways, cloakrooms, and verandas were adapted into work-bays and display areas, while communicating links were provided between classrooms. Resulting from these changes, new forms of organization such as team teaching, cooperative teaching, vertical grouping, and the integrated day have emerged.

Team teaching is a teaching organization in which two or more teachers are responsible for teaching a given set of pupils. The organization may take many forms and differ according to the availability of teachers and required needs. The principle is for teachers *with a common philosophy* to group together. The grouping may involve teachers of equal status with designated responsibilities or a team with an appointed leader. The leader usually will be a senior member of staff with less experienced teachers as her team. The coordinator has the task of organizing the team into an efficient teaching force. This she may do by allocating responsibility to each member either by year groups or by subjects.

Team teaching is criticized as a less personal system that weakens pupil/teacher interaction. Children become attached to their teacher in the class teacher system. She becomes a trusted figure on whom they can rely. The situation is not the same with three or four teachers sharing the onus as divided loyalties towards teachers may develop. A charismatic teacher may overshadow other teachers and destroy the basis of teamwork, or a teacher who does not delegate sufficiently, is critical of her colleagues or a bad organizer could unbalance the team and encourage children to take sides. The children may become confused if varying degrees of teacher expectation exist. The fundamental considerations of team teaching are organization, the age of the children in the groups, and whether to integrate or specialize curriculum content. Specialization is more suitable to older primary school children than younger children and, may be a way to wean children from the complete freedom of an open situation to a closed one which will be desirable a year or two later when they attend secondary school.

An alternative with younger children is to adopt cooperative teaching; an organization that is often confused with team teaching. Cooperative teaching occurs when two teachers join forces. One teacher may be experienced and the other newly qualified, but there is no attempt to specialize. Although one teacher may assume overall responsibility for mathematics and the other reading, the children are free to approach either teacher for the subjects. The teachers pool their efforts, and work alongside each other. The organization encourages greater flexibility for teachers and children. One teacher may associate with a small group of children with their mathematics work, while her colleague is reading a story to the remaining children. Next day, the tasks may be reversed. Children with special needs are able to be looked after by one of the teachers. These children are with their own teacher, unlike children who are withdrawn from their class for 'remedial' work with another teacher. The success or failure of cooperative teaching depends upon the harmony between the teachers. Many two teacher village schools, and nursery schools, have worked in this way for a number of years and, when understanding exists between the teachers concerned, larger schools should cope just as efficiently.

Arranging children in year groups is the most common practice in primary schools but, owing to an uneven distribution of ages, many village schools organize classes across age-bands. Some Infants' Schools adopt a similar procedure which is known as vertical or family grouping. Infants' Schools have termly intakes but an annual output, so provisions have to be made for children admitted after the Christmas and Easter holidays. Children already in school are removed to other classes to free a teacher to form a new reception class. To avoid this upheaval, vertically grouped classes contain children whose ages spread across two or three years so new entrants are absorbed into the existing classes. The theory is that these children should settle more easily into school by mixing with children who are accustomed to the routines of the class and school; especially if the class contains an older brother or sister. The teacher should be able to concentrate on the new entrants as she has fewer of them than if she had a whole class, and the older children should not make as many demands on her. The system should also aid older, under-achieving children as they are able to mix with the younger children without sense of failure.

Disadvantages may accrue from vertical grouping. As the custom is for the same children to remain with the same teacher throughout their Infants' School years, the practice limits children's contact with other adults, and could be detrimental if a child and teacher did not get on with each other, or if the teacher happened to be weak. Some younger children may be overshadowed by the older children, or they may imitate them and acquire undesirable learning habits or behaviour patterns.

Vertical grouping is associated mostly with Infants' Schools, but it is possible to apply the system in junior schools, and even to incorporate it with team teaching or cooperative teaching. This involves merging year groups, but such a practice is questionable. The groups could be used to assign children by ability and attainment, and imply a return to the Standards used in the elementary school days.

Many vital factors must be considered when contemplating team teaching, cooperative teaching or vertical grouping organizations. The ultimate decision to implement them rests with the head teacher and this emphasizes the power of his position. With a 'wave of his hand', he could change the organization of his school overnight and so affect children's school careers. Although he has autonomy in decisions which relate to organization within his school, a wise head teacher will seek the feelings and agreement of his staff before making changes. It cannot be ignored that these changes will be influenced by the type of school building, but pressure from outside the school in the form of Education Officers, advisers, Her Majesty's Inspectors, parents, society, and educational fashion may influence his decision.

Education in primary schools in recent years has been one of change. Heads and teachers have been encouraged in this direction by theories, educationalists, books, articles, courses, advisers, and new school buildings; the emphasis being development. Teachers have acquiesced to the demands as promotion prospects hinge on whether they keep abreast with developments but limited attention has been given to the educational principles which should emanate from theoretical expositions. Frequently, teachers have had a minimum grasp of what they were attempting. Now, the very people who have encouraged development are accusing teachers of inadequate standards. Although teachers may be blamed for not becoming better educationalists, much of the blame rests with those who perpetrated changes without making adequate provisions for teachers to be prepared to undertake new ways of teaching, and who advocated open plan schools because of lower building costs.

Whoever is to blame, there are now many open plan schools, and questions to be asked of team teaching, cooperative teaching, and vertical grouping and their influence on mixed ability teaching. What provisions are made for high and low achieving children? If children are grouped according to ability, is this not streaming? If, within team teaching, children are set according to their ability in subjects, is this not streaming? Therefore, are adequate provisions for children as individuals being made within the organizations? How is the curriculum evaluated, and assessment made of children's achievements? If there are curriculum objectives, ways must be devised to ensure that teaching is geared towards them. This emphasizes the need to keep profiles of children's attainments, otherwise who is to know how they are progressing?

Teaching is more difficult in an open plan school than a closed classroom. Teachers could spend time trying to locate the whereabouts of children instead of teaching. This would indicate a lack of curriculum design as no-one had planned the organization of the complex, or was working towards specific aims. Open plan teaching needs a structure with each teacher knowing what and how she is to do things throughout the day. This requires careful planning and consultation between teachers; normally every day. A consistent routine is essential if children are to be familiar with the organization and become organized themselves. In short, qualities of excellence are fundamental in any teaching situation and, to ensure that they are being obtained, curriculum evaluation is crucial. With complex organizations which team teaching, cooperative teaching, and vertical grouping may promote, evaluation is most important to ascertain that all is well.

Mixed ability teaching is not confined to open plan schools. In older primary schools which retain the closed classroom with a single teacher, non-streaming has become the most favoured form of organization. This, too, could present problems for a teacher. Throughout the age-range of the primary school — five to eleven years — children range from pre-operational thought to abstract thought. The band spreads wider as children progress up the school. At five years of age, a class of children will cluster around the stages of pre-operational and intuitive thought but, by eleven years of age, some children may have just entered concrete thought while others will be coping with abstract problems.

To facilitate easier management, and provide time to deal with children individually or in groups, teachers may institute an integrated day but the term has caused misunderstanding and confusion in primary schools. It is often applied incorrectly to the integration of curriculum content and, at an extreme, a situation when children do as they like. The integrated day merely describes the school day as being open without stratification by time-tabled sections. Children then have the option of when to undertake their various activities. The integrated day may be incorporated into any organization apart from the entire day, specified lesson approach. Circumstances within a school do not allow every class, or group of children, to have absolute freedom of choice as restrictions of certain school areas must be considered in the planning of the day. The school hall needs to be time-tabled for assembly, physical education, movement, country dancing, etc., a specified time is necessary for swimming and games, and a class may be following a television programme which is transmitted at a particular time.

Allowing for these exigencies, the integrated day may take several forms, but eventually is determined by the organization of the school and the mode preferred by the teacher. Moreover, children cannot be expected to be plunged into an integrated day. Such attempts have caused dis-integration of the curriculum in some schools. To institute an integrated day successfully requires explicit, and detailed planning. The children should be shown how to organize themselves, be acquainted with what is expected of them, be clear of the areas around the school in which they may work, be conversant of how to go about their work, be made aware of when work assignments are expected to be completed, and be conscious of the responsibilities entrusted to them. As such, the integrated day places responsibilities on children for the care of equipment, tidiness, and sharing with others. The organization does not mean a commitment to ceaseless noise, uncontrolled activity or haphazard teaching. The teacher instils the behaviour pattern which she expects, and the organization, itself, does much to engender a conducive atmosphere in a classroom, work bay, etc.

The planning of an integrated day is described by Choat (1971). Initially, the children were grouped according to an aspect of a project they desired to follow. Each group was designated when it could undertake various activities during the day. After four weeks, the children had accustomed themselves to the organization, what was expected of them, and their responsibilities, for a more flexible system to be introduced. Then, the children were able to choose how they organized the day, with whom they worked, where they worked, and the activities which they undertook, but they were committed to some written work, reading and mathematics each day. An alternative pattern is explained by Palmer (1969). History, geography and science are combined in long, block periods to give children time to be 'absorbed untrammelled by subject boundaries' with free choice periods each day or several times a week.

Whatever form the integrated day may take, children should not be expected to continue indefinitely with individual work. Apart from class lessons being desirable on occasions, and allowing for children to socialize by mixing in groups, a need remains to exemplify that they are members of a community. Class sessions are valuable to permit children to deliberate on their findings, to read their written work to the rest of the class, to question each other, to encourage qualities of excellence in English and correct faults, and discuss future phases in inquiry. Literature, in the form of a story read in instalments, or individual stories for younger children, add to the corporate spirit when the whole class joins together to share in a common experience.

The integrated day encourages children to develop thought and extend experience. The relaxed atmosphere of the classroom stimulates learning. As children gain confidence in their own capabilities, the work output often exceeds expectations with qualities of excellence above those originally envisaged. The children foresake their breaks and lunch times and stay behind after school to continue with activities. Nevertheless, the vital component of the integrated day is the role taken by the teacher. Children cannot be expected to work individually or in groups, seek activites, and pursue inquiries unless there is association with the teacher. The teacher's task is to ensure that children are working to their ability, have an understanding of what they are doing, and that learning is productive. Children, too, want an ultimate goal and someone who will appreciate their efforts to reach the goal.

Mixed ability teaching encourages the integrated day, but the integrated day fosters mixed ability teaching by providing time for individual attention and teaching small groups. Nevertheless, the two organizations are not restricted to each other. An integrated day is as easily operated with a streamed class. Irrespectivce of children being categorized as 'A', 'B', or 'C', marked differences in capability exist, and the need for individual and group teaching remains. Labelling children as the same instils blanket teaching of a whole class. The flexibility of the integrated day encourages integration of curriculum content. In schools with a fixed time-table, each subject is separately identified and allocated a fixed time when it is to be taught. The integrated day dispenses with rigid time-tabling and compartmentalization of subjects. Instead, it allows centres of interest and projects which integrate curriculum content.

The centre of interest, as its name implies, is pursuing a particular interest. The system is followed mostly in Infants' Schools when a teacher selects a title, e.g. the postman, trains, hamsters, trees, etc., and encourages children to participate in the development of class displays, paintings, written work, etc. The teacher connects the title by stories, songs, models, and discussion but in most instances the essential elements of play, creative activities, reading, writing, and mathematics are not displaced. The criterion of the centre of interest is to provide a stimulating influence within the classroom for a week, month or longer, but it is not continued once children's interest begins to wane.

The project is associated more with the junior school. Theoretically, the project may emanate from either the teacher or the children and arise from interest, experience or a happening, but more often than not the teacher deliberately chooses an area of investigation. There should not be preconceived notions of what the project is attempting, but most teachers have a definite direction in view. Once the area of inquiry is resolved, the resultant activities should branch out as and when they occur. In her role as guide and director of the operation, the teacher must make preliminary plans of where branches are likely to lead, but remain flexible within the planning. The initial planning allows for an analysis and dissemination of the project, and the preparation of books, materials, visits, etc., but these are only a framework of possible directions. Once the project is under way, the teacher should be prepared to elaborate leads and amend her original plans if the occasion arises.

To take an example, the chosen project may be 'The Docks'. Ideally, the children should be taken on a visit to the docks to see at first hand what happens there, but frequently this is not possible. Instead, the teacher plots the various avenues of inquiry. These will most likely form sub-areas which various groups of children will pursue, and may consist of the work of the docks, how the docks originated, identification of various jobs, investigating how the cranes and other machinery work, refrigeration on ships, different cargoes on ships, where the ships and their cargoes come from, how the ships get to the docks, the work of ships' pilots, life on board a ship, the duties and responsibilities of a ship's captain, storms at sea, rescues at sea, how ships navigate, and how ships are repaired. Development could be endless but from their inquiries children will be expected to produce paintings, models, poems, descriptive and creative writing, etc.

Specialization by subjects is not a prerogative of a project as the emphasis is general inquiry by the children. Moreover, once the project is being pursued, the recognition of subjects is not easy, but children need proficiency in various subjects before they are able to benefit from their inquiries. They need to be able to read to acquire facts, be proficient in writing and spelling to give legible accounts of the findings, be able to draw, paint and make models, and use mathematics on many occasions. Some teachers will contend that a project enables proficiency in subjects to be developed, but is this possible when a child is deficient in the foundations of the subject? If the project is open-ended there is a danger that some children will concentrate on narrow areas of inquiry, i.e. where the ships and their cargoes come from. This does little for a child who has not acquired the 'numberness of number'.

A project does not guarantee a balance of curriculum content. It is possible that children may not encounter certain subjects, or other subjects may be over-emphasized. In some schools the quality of 'free' writing is high but no corresponding effort is made in mathematics. Roaming across a wide range of subject areas does not ensure that children can relate one aspect to another. Children's interests are erratic. They may inquire into one area of the project but become tired of it. Curriculum objectives should include attention to individual children's progression in various subjects. Management of a project, and the integration of content are skilful operations for a teacher if each child in a mixed ability class is to achieve according to his capability. Demands are made on the teacher if she is to ensure that this is so, and it requires knowledge and expertise. Integrated work may easily degenerate into aimless pursuits which have little educational value in the hands of an incompetent teacher. Ideas may be followed without relevance to learning, activites undertaken for no apparent reason, and discoveries explored for no useful purpose. Specialization eliminates doubt, and gives children a more thorough preparation in specific subjects but this should not be taken as a rejection of inter-disciplinary work. Under the direction of a capable teacher, and if the function of education is to organize, accelerate, and direct the process of learning to produce individuals who will contribute to the fitness of society, the project has much to offer. A teacher is able to cater for the needs and interests of individual children. In a mixed ability class, she is in a position to encourage academic and social integration between children and foster greater association between the children and herself to enhance learning and develop communication. She has the opportunity to present challenge to the more able children while making provisions for the less able. This could mean specifying different objectives in the sense that each child is determining his own objectives by his approach to work, and that the objectives are fluctuating according to his development. As such, teacher expectations of children's outcomes are fluid. Above all, a teacher should be providing challenge in children through experiences to bring about learning. This emphasizes that within content integration children should be able to practise the concepts and skills which have been acquired previously, but development is at a standstill unless provisions are made for progression. Although integration of content through a project may be the accepted form of teaching, development in specific subject areas must be recognized by the teacher.

However interesting project work may be, and however occupied some children may appear, it cannot be attempted unless the teacher has formulated possible outcomes for the children. Integration of curriculum content is complex and raises the question of whether every teacher is capable of undertaking the task or whether specialization may be desirable in some circumstances and for some subjects. A second language, usually French, taught by film strips and tape cassettes cannot be incorporated into a project. Music, if it is to be taught properly, must be undertaken by a person capable of transmitting feeling for the subject. A case, too, could be made for art and creative work for a teacher who is unable to give expression herself is unlikely to stimulate children. Likewise, physical education is required to be taken by every primary school teacher and would benefit from specialization. The identification of children's progress must be considered whatever the form of organization, and this could present problems if not catered for within an integration of content. The Bullock Report (1975, p.200-206) emphasizes that some teachers find it difficult to give sufficient help with reading on an individual basis when they are pulled in so many directions. They allege some classes which followed the integrated day were less imaginative and demanding than more formal classes. When children moved to the language bay, they would take an assignment card and work to the given instructions. The Report does not hesitate to say that some of the conventions of language need to be taught, not necessarily to a full class, but taught none the less, and later (p.222), although referring to secondary schools, 'we cannot emphasize too strongly the need for strong specialist representation where English is part of an integrated programme, whatever form this may take'. The Report regards the opposition between specialized English and integrated studies as a false issue for it is evading fundamentals to consider them as mutually exclusive as specialist areas exist whether they remain separate or are 'folded into' others, and a school has to decide what its objectives are for each.

Most subject specialists would make a case for their own subject being treated preferentially within an integration of content. Present-day culture is understood better by an acquisition of events from the past, thereby history stimulates the imagination of children to increase their appraisals of man and his exploits. Geography is the foundation upon which may be built sensitive and accurate imagining about strange lands and customs (Plowden Report, 1967, p.230), and is the means whereby children assess potentialities of their neighbourhoods. Nature study has always been a feature of the primary school with children studying things at first hand through their natural interests in animals, birds, plants and insects, but in addition to these biological aspects physical science also plays an active role in the lives of children. Religious education, the only compulsory subject in schools, will be claimed by many specialists as the means for setting the tone of living and learning for the school community, but, with increasing concern being given to multi-ethnic education, the study of comparative religions will enable older children in primary schools to appreciate other people's beliefs.

Although each subject can be identified separately, each is dependent on mathematics in some form or other for its understanding. In reading, a child needs to be able to recognize and differentiate between the shapes of letters, distinguish the space between words, and select one word from others. Language development, as illustrated by the Bullock Report (*op. cit.,* pp. 47-50), is classification through the use of sets with hierarchial development occurring through inclusion when flowers are used to demonstrate grouping into classes. When writing, a child needs to employ shape, size, distance, order, and symbols in his control of a pencil to coordinate his hand, brain, and eye responses. These capabilities result from varied experiences which develop a child's conceptualization of space, shape, size, order, distance, neighbourhoods, positions, categorization, classification, sorting, matching, corresponding, grouping, and sets to determine the patterns of relationship. In geography, a child is constantly referring to aspects of spatial relationships. In science, he depends on mathematics for calculations, measuring, and weighing. Movement in space, seriation, order, position, and distance are integral to physical education. Music derives from its notation and thereby employs the mathematical notions of relationships, neighbourhoods, and order. Children constantly refer to mathematics when they undertake art and craft and in particular symmetry and geometry.

Mathematics is implicit in almost everything in which primary school children are involved. If the aim of the primary school curriculum is to offer experiences to children that will explain their world to them through using their ability to awaken an interest in the relevance of mathematics to life, to define patterns and relationships, to ask questions, interpret actions, and develop a tenacity and will to further inquiries then a mathematically inspired curriculum is desirable. If, as the Bullock Report (*op. cit.,* pp. 188-91), claims, there is justification for a language policy across the curriculum, so validity exists for a mathematics policy across the curriculum. A mathematical education promotes values which are essential if children are to lead a full and active life through its own practical uses, by being a cultural subject which leads children to come to terms with the world, as a part of their basic language through which they are able to interpret and communicate with others, and by encouraging logical and ordered thought. The assertion was made previously that curriculum principles would not be interpreted by primary school teachers until they appreciated the relevance of these values to the whole of the curriculum. It cannot be otherwise if mathematics is everywhere and in almost everything. This complicates the specialization/integration issue, and raises pertinent aspects concerning a teacher's treatment of mathematics in her overall view of the curriculum.

The teacher must decide how she is to provide for continuity in mathematical learning, the organization of the class irrespective of mixed ability, and whether mathematical progression can be identified within an integration of curriculum content. Dearden (1976, pp.41-7) insists that mathematics warrants special attention if integration is practised as, left to chance, mathematical problems will not arise from other interests in a systematic way either in the right order, at the right level of difficulty, with provision for enough practice, or at the right time. Watson (1976, pp. 129-30) has the same opinion. Admitting that the links between mathematics and other subjects have not been very energetically explored in the past, he is concerned that within integration mathematics could lose its separate identity and be completely submerged with the danger that the links within mathematics would be neglected. Watson considers that the explanatory power of mathematics resides largely in the way many situations are recognized to be similar. It seems probable to Watson that the coherence and cross-linking which are essential to mathematical understanding necessitate some separate consideration of the subject.

Gardner, Glenn and Renton (1973, pp. 116-22) maintain that mathematics does not naturally arise from a project. Their contention is difficult to follow as they frequently misinterpret integrated day, integrated content, topic and project, assume that an integrated day must involve an integration of content, and refer to topics (the following of an area of investigation by defined subjects) when they mean project. Nevertheless, they uphold that failures are likely to occur in the development of mathematical knowledge as the progression of concepts and processes may be distorted in modern approaches to teaching. Gardener *et al.* does not doubt that many areas of investigation are rich enough in mathematical ideas to meet the needs of primary school children, and would generate mathematics if only teachers were sufficiently aware of the possibilities. To illustrate their contention, they add that children can find out adequately enough what domestic life was like a century ago without first investigating life a hundred years earlier. But, they contend, children cannot master the process of division without first being familiar with multiplication. Many primary school teachers, particularly those who are historians, would disagree with Gardner *et al.* and insist that the prior period of history makes the latter period relevant. On the other hand, many educationalists maintain that teaching should begin with the known and then proceed to the unknown. This means that a project should begin with domestic life during the present day. Moreover, why should children be taught multiplication and division separately? Good mathematics teaching should emphasize reversibility of the operations.

Project work to Gardner *et al.* is rich enough to contain adequate mathematics. Even when 'number work' is readily available, they feel that the 'quantitative' element is forced into a situation rather than 'abstracted' from it. For a project to be successful in developing quantitative skills and knowledge, they consider it must:

1. contain situations from which mathematics may be drawn and subsequently developed;
2. contain situations to which mathematics already known may be applied;
3. require or give rise to mathematics at the appropriate level of development.

With the addition of concepts to be acquired from the project, most primary school teachers would agree with Gardner *et al.,* who adds that a project which does not meet both (3) and either (1) or (2), however valuable in other ways to children, is of very little use to their mathematical development. They recommend that even in the most smoothly run schools time should be set aside for specific work in mathematics, and stipulate four objectives:

1. To practise skills that have emerged from or have been required by the work of any project;
2. To fill up gaps in knowledge that must inevitably occur in situations that have not been specifically planned to yield connected account of a mathematical topic;
3. Reconsider the mathematical work that has been done in a suitable sequence, either logical or pedagogic, so that the child can grasp its development;
4. Extend the work mathematically, adding in topics that have not emerged from the given project or situations so that knowledge becomes systematic. Until it becomes systematic it is not mathematics.

Again Gardner *et al.* ignor conceptualization, and seem to hold a view that mathematical development is linear. This is contrary to Choat (1977) who suggests that mathematical development is partially-ordered with children returning, through activities and experiences, to lower order concepts for interpretation before higher order concepts are acquired. Undoubtedly, teachers should possess a systematic knowledge of mathematics but to impose this view on children is no more than stipulating a common curriculum and removing individuality in a mixed ability class. Mathematical concepts cannot be taught but are abstracted from a variety of experiences. The acquisition of concepts must go hand in hand with skills for neither is much use without the other, so a teacher's task is to provide a suitably balanced diet of both. Matthews (1973) maintains that it is not easy to divorce mathematics from other subjects in the first two years of a child's school life, but the teacher must be aware of the progression in mathematical concepts in order to provide materials, opportunities, and experiences required by a child to help him acquire the early concepts.

Sime (1977) claims that projects enable the mathematically minded teacher to exploit mathematical learning to the full, while other teachers leave a project completely empty of mathematics, or even empty of reasoning at all, and make it a culling together of material facts. She illustrates her contention with an example of two teachers who separately took classes to visit a small dock. One class, armed with clip boards and pencils, asked innumerable prepared questions, wrote many statements and figures, and went back to school to present in essay form with a few paintings and a random shaped model of the dock. The other class, also with clip boards, took measuring tools including a small home-made plane table. They measured the dock, the buildings, containers of all shapes, and workings of the cranes and dock gates. They, too, asked questions and took home answers, but followed up with a whole term's valuable, mathematically reasoned work that overlapped into economics.

Just as Dearden (*op. cit.*), Watson (*op. cit.*) and Gardner *et al.* (*op. cit.*) are insistent that mathematics should be identified within an integration of content so Kohl (1977 pp.54-75) insists that it should not. He alleges that different subject areas are kept separate at the cost of diminishing what may be learned. Kohl considers that when subjects are differentiated no attempt is made to relate them to each other, or to follow ways in which man comes to know and live with himself and the environment. Children get the impression that science is one thing and art something totally different. This is attributed to text books and teachers' manuals which enforce fragmentation of learning as teachers depend on them to move from one area to another. Thinking and creating in science, the arts, and mathematics are not that different according to Kohl. There are mathematicians whose thoughts are essentially poetic, and poets whose works are mathematical. There are degrees of intuition, rationality, boldness, caution, grandness, or meticulousness in all creative thinkers. The more schools separate areas of thought, the more they encourage children not to think in any of them. It is not difficult to bring curriculum content together to break down the barriers between subject areas.

Irrespective of these ideals, Kohl becomes confused when later he advocates that teachers should be prepared to teach basic skills in reading, writing and mathematics no matter what age children they work with or subject they teach. He recommends teachers who are uneasy with mathematics to learn from children by discovering what games they play, how they deal with money, how they divide things among themselves, and how they measure food. From this informal knowledge, Kohl suggests moving to more abstract mathematics by devising a mathematical progression or referring to a teachers' manual which emphasizes child centred mathematical development. Such action is hardly in keeping with his earlier pronouncements.

These views of mathematics within an integration of content

illustrate the complexity surrounding the issue, and involve returning to the controversy between objectives and psychology in mathematics teaching. The suggestion is not that specialists are advocating instrumental learning nor denying that provisions have to be made to ensure mathematical progression, but that clarification of the issue is clouded by insisting on objectives without considering how mathematics is learned by children. Mathematicians who demand specialization disregard psychological factors in their pursuit of objectives, and in doing so disregard children as individuals. The prime consideration should be how the objectives relate to individual children, 'why' mathematics is taught, 'how' it is taught, and 'what' is taught. Commenting on the article referred to in the Introduction, Leslie A. Smith states that the various disciplines, each with its own private language, might become richer still if they could, at times, inter-relate within the context of dialogue between specialists of varying persuasions, and the varying degrees of mastery over the views each discipline presents. Smith adds that the bases of mathematics explored in the primary school illustrate the way an apparent random study can be turned to good account at the secondary stage; but, and he maintains that it is an important 'but', the work involved is possessed of immense complexity.

The issue requires a recapitulation of the deliberations of the preceding chapters. If mathematics is the key to the primary school curriculum, attention must be paid to the consequences of the effect. This emphasizes the need to define the purpose of the curriculum, what is meant and what is intended with rational assumptions to evolve teaching strategies which make allowances for children of mixed ability. Thereby, realistic objectives are able to be specified; objectives which may be attained through the inherent logic of the subject matter and which ensure that the teaching and learning processes keep in step with children's levels of psychological development. The degree to which children aspire in mathematics is dependent largely on the psychological factors of ability, intelligence, perception, abstraction, motivation, and play, and how these factors relate at any given time to the task involved.

Children gain experiences through activities and the richness of the activities determines the richness of the experiences. With their curiosity to explore, they constantly meet situations which are predominantly spatial, and have an urge to manipulate and control these situations. Through geometry they build up a collection of logical systems. These logical, geometric relationships are accessible for use in non-geometric situations, and encourage discrimination and generalization to develop the ability to see other relationships, recognize correspondences, sort into classifications, and order experiences.

Transfer from concrete thought to abstract thought is facilitated by experiences when children exercise their perceptual powers, and remove by representation to abstracting. The formation of concepts does not necessarily arise through play or any other activity. Conceptualization occurs only when abstraction of originals are made through representation by image and thought. Symbolic play permits representation but it is the manner in which the representation is rationalized that specifies the extent of conceptualization, and hence, thought.

Consequently, children should be offered play and other experiences that, through conceptualization, will develop an understanding to cope sensibly with life, but the curriculum should also explain their world to children. To do this, curriculum planners are dependent on mathematics if the subject is recognized as the science of space and number in the abstract, and the medium whereby children discern and record the structures of their world through the study of systematic patterns of relationship. Mathematics has an effect on the curriculum that cannot be ignored. Even when integration of curriculum content is favoured, progression in mathematics determines progression in other subjects as children are reliant on mathematics for much of their understanding in the subjects. A teacher's attitude to her teaching of mathematics determines her attitude to her teaching generally with a definition of the curriculum and elucidation of her objectives, organization and method. Resolving these, means specifying to a teacher her own standing in children's learning and her role as associate or otherwise. From these attitudinal effects, the motivational level of the class is established and this depends upon the stimulus aroused by the teacher, and her degree of expectation. She will acknowledge that patterns of expectation vary in a class of mixed ability, but that satisfactory outcomes are obtained only by fitting mathematics to children.

Irrespective of specialization or integration of mathematics in the primary school, the principles of teaching mathematics must be re-emphasized:

1. A framework within which a teacher is able to implement learning situations for children to reach desired outcomes;

2. The recognition of the importance of understanding in the sense of ensuring that the inherent logic of a mathematical activity is grasped, and in the sense of ensuring that both the teaching and learning processes are in step with children's psychological stages of development;

3. Although learning is a continuous process, children vary in their ability and in the extent to which their attitude to learning is affected by social, emotional, physical and intellectual factors, and

4. Although children may have freedom to be active and to inquire, assistance is needed to translate actions, and this comes about by association with the teacher.

Interpretation of these principles by a teacher determines how she caters for children of mixed ability, and the teaching techniques which she employs. Method is often confused with organization but organization is the systematic structure that enables learning to take place, and method is the means employed by a teacher whereby interaction between the learner and some other person, object, or experience takes place to bring about learning. Learning is a measurable change that involves either the acquisition of some new body of information (cognition learning) or a shift in values, attitudes, interests, or motivation (non-cognitive learning). Consequently, learning may cover many different activities that, although they have the common characteristic of a change in behaviour, are radically different and, are elaborated by Thouless (1969) as 1. the acquisition of information by mechanical remembering, 2. the acquisition of information by logical remembering, 3. the acquisition of certain bodily skills, 4. the acquisition of a number of intellectual skills, and 5. the acquisition of a certain group of desirable or obligatory attitudes that include aesthetic, social, and moral attitudes.

Presentation of learning means what a teacher does to bring about learning in children. The success of methods depends upon the stimulation offered, the degree to which the content and materials have been analysed as suitable to the level of development, and the manner in which learning is presented. In her attempt to accrue motivation in her pupils, a teacher should consider whether she has specified the correct sequences and stages of content appropriate to children's needs, and whether the children will be interested in, and able to understand, her teaching presentation. It is pointless for a teacher to devise an elaborate teaching technique with either structural apparatus, a visit to the surrounding neighbourhood, etc. that is beyond children' level of development, is too involved, or if the subject matter is boring. Method must relate to children's needs and interests if curriculum objectives are to be attained, and an awareness of the most suitable presentation if needs are to be met. These implications return to a teacher's expectations as the selected method will depend on what the teacher has resolved as her anticipated outcomes. This, in turn, focusses attention to teacher/pupil relationships and classroom atmosphere for these are dependent on the reciprocity and association which the teacher is prepared to give to learning.

Attempts have been made to categorize teaching styles, and the most quoted definitions are those of Lippitt and White (1943). The study refers to youth club leadership, but its relevance to classrooms is important. Three categories of styles are defined. The authoritarian climate is teacher-centred with formal teaching, teacher directed communication, a high incidence of competitiveness and convergent thinking by pupils. The *laissez-faire* climate is in complete contrast, with the teacher playing an inactive role and the children being left to their own devices. Between the two extremes, the democratic climate is learner-centred with concern for the individual needs of each child and stress on cooperation, verbal and physical activity, and socialization.

The democratic classroom with an emphasis on pupil participation is more likely to involve children in individual and group teaching methods than the other styles of teaching, but methods may vary from teacher to teacher. In some classes, children will read individually to the teacher, but in other classes a group of children may be reading the same book and, after a chapter has been read, the teacher will question the children on their comprehension of the passage. In mathematics, the children may work individually with teaching given when necessary, or be grouped according to levels of development. The latter organization is a form of streaming but it enables children to cooperate and allows economy of time for a teacher.

The method most appropriate to a particular activity or experience will then be applied by the teacher. The most common practice in the past was verbal description with the aid of the blackboard, 'chalk and talk', and was followed by the pupils doing work in their books. The method is still essential to present day teaching but with a small group of children instead of the whole class, and the teacher may use a large sheet of paper instead of the blackboard. Discussion either individually or with a group of children is integral to learning. The inadequate language of many children reinforces the desirability to encourage speech within classrooms. As an alternative to direct teaching, the primary school teacher may present children with an activity which involves inquiry. For example, a variety of blocks will be available for children to find how many of each size of block respond to a certain weight. A further method involves the use of assignment cards which give children specific instructions. These can be useful to consolidate previous learning, e.g. if the children have been concerned with measuring length, the assignment card can specify a further activity, but the card must be clear and precise, and within the capabilities of the children concerned. Text books, too, used wisely, are still a means from which children can work.

Individual and group methods create a demand for more and different kinds of materials. A teacher should take into account the apparatus which has been in existence for some time as well as more recent innovations. The blackboard, visual aid, flannel graph, slide projector, film projector, radio, television, record player and tape recorder are established ancillaries but new devices such as teaching machines, loop projectors, desk and hand calculators, and structural apparatus have entered primary schools. However useful these aids may be, none of them is able to replace a teacher. Her association in learning situations is most important to children.

Play and the environment in children's acquisition of mathematics has been implicit throughout this book, but their usefulness as teaching methods is often overlooked, or even rejected, by many teachers. Play is regarded by some teachers as the prerogative of nursery and Infants' schools, but this is not the case as play is as important with older primary school children as with younger children. Teachers like to think that they can transplant their own thoughts into the minds of children by explanation, but the response is negative if the children are unable to conceptualize at the required level. With an opportunity to play with materials to investigate properties, and to employ logico-mathematical deductions to discern patterns of relationship, children are abstracting to build mental models prior to undertaking a directed task. Through play many older primary school children are able to understand something which would be unrecognizable in a more formal teaching method.

The environment which children experience in school is manufactured by their teacher. She is responsible for providing the activities through which learning takes place. Consequently, the richness of the environment depends on the teacher's degree of preparation and awareness of opportunities at her disposal. When determining her teaching method, a teacher should be conscious of the mathematics inherent in any activity as the environment is formulated largely through mathematics. The aspect re-asserts that the attitude taken by the teacher to mathematics determines her attitude to the curriculum, and her teaching methods.

This definition of environment is contrary to the general description of 'using the environment' as a teaching method. In this context, environment is vague; sometimes meaning the influence of home, parents and family, patterns of behaviour of social groups, or an exploration of the surrounding neighbourhood through a project or centre of interest. A project provides opportunities for the development of children as persons to see the world objectively, but this is of no avail unless the teacher applies environment in its realistic sense by providing for learning from which understanding will be extracted. The distinction is (a) a surface appraisal of gathering material facts when 'using the environment' or (b) a 'learning environment' (which may include the surroundings) that is conducive to cognition, values, attitudes, needs, interests, and motivation.

Teaching methods demand a great deal of thought by a teacher, and this is particularly true of mathematics and its relevance to the primary school curriculum. Choat (1978, pp.57-8) explains that in a mixed ability class some children may have learned their tables of multiplication, be conversant with the operations on number, have a thorough knowledge of the properties of shapes, etc., while other children may still be attempting to acquire the 'numberness of number'. The teacher must systematize provisions for the more able children to develop from their existing level of development and plan activities for the less able. The reluctance of some teachers to equip themselves to teach in this way, the failure by others to come to grips with what is required, and the acceptance of a minority for 'an easy way out' encourage the adoption of selected sets of text books that are followed slavishly and which impose behavioural objectives. However convenient this method may be, it does not ensure mathematical progression for children. The situation in some schools is for children to work through a series of work books which accompany the mathematics scheme. A danger exists with such an arrangement of children working blindly through the work books and not knowing what they are doing. Such a practice is disastrous if treated in isolation from developmental factors whereby concept acquisition is recognized with resultant understanding being used in the practice of skills. The adoption of particular forms of structural apparatus, and the insistence on specific approaches to mathematics, e.g. Cuisenaire, Biggs, Nuffield, Dienes, etc. may have equally unsatisfactory results. Repeatedly using the same apparatus in the same way does not expand children's experiences. They merely repeat the same processes and eventually resort to learning by rote. These approaches have each, in their own way, contributed something to assist teachers, but there is only one way to teach mathematics satisfactorily. Teachers must define how they are to cater for progression for each child in their class by bearing in mind levels of development and the pace of learning.

This way of teaching dispenses with prescribed standards, and permits children to attain in mathematics to a level determined by capability. Teachers are not restricted to concentrate on computation on number and exclude the remainder of mathematics; they have flexibility to cater for the needs of children. Nevertheless, a teacher may set out with good intentions but be forced to revert to formal methods by pressures brought about by the management of a mixed ability class, i.e. her inability to structure opportunities for learning. Likewise, the vocabulary associated with teaching — needs, interests, levels of development, the child as an individual, flexibility of teaching, integrated day, integration of content, child-centred, etc. may obscure curriculum objectives. The adoption of mixed ability teaching should not lull a teacher into complacency or to possess an abstract ideology. The primary school curriculum should be learner-centred with recognition of the role that mathematics plays within learning. Such a contention diminishes the argument of whether the curriculum should be child-centred, knowledge-centred or a social ideal. A combination of each is needed to attain degrees of excellence and, only when teachers appreciate this and implement it in their teaching, will primary school children achieve according to their capability.

References

CHOAT, E. (1971). 'Introducing the Integrated Day in Junior School', *Forum in Education*, **13**, 3, 89-90.

CHOAT, E. (1977). 'The Relative Development in Young Children of Geometrical and Numerical Concepts', *Educational Studies*, **3**, 2, 153-69.

CHOAT, E. (1978). *Children's Acquisition of Mathematics*. Windsor: NFER Publishing Company.

DEARDEN, R.F. (1976). *Problems in Primary Education*. London: Routledge & Kegan Paul.

DEPARTMENT OF EDUCATION AND SCIENCE (1975). *A Language for Life*. (The Bullock Report). London: HMSO.

GARDNER, K.L., GLENN, J.A., and RENTON, A.I.G. (1973). *Children Using Mathematics*. London: Oxford University Press.

KOHL, H. (1977). *On Teaching*. London: Methuen.

LIPPITT, R. and WHITE, R.K. (1943). 'The Social Climate of Children's Groups'. In: BARKER, E.G. (Ed) *Child Behaviour and Development*. New York: McGraw Hill.

MATTHEWS, J. (1973). 'Learning, Organization and Recording in the Infant School'. In: CHOAT, E. (Ed) *Pre-School and Primary Mathematics*. London: Ward Lock Educational.

PALMER, R. (1969). 'Degrees of Structure in the Learning Situation', *Occasional Papers in Primary Education*, No. 15. London: ILEA.

Report of the CONSULTATIVE COMMITTEE ON THE PRIMARY SCHOOL. (1931). (The Hadow Report). London: HMSO.

Report of the CENTRAL ADVISORY COUNCIL FOR EDUCATION (ENGLAND) (1967) *Children and their Primary Schools* (The Plowden Report). London: HMSO.

SIME, M. (1977). 'Some Excellent Applications and Unfortunate Distortions of Attempts to Relate Piagetian Theory to Teaching Mathematics', *The New Era*, **58**, 5, 125-9.

SMITH, L.A. (1977). 'Ideas (Editorial)', *The New Era*, **58**, 5, 111-2.

THOULESS, R.H. (1969). *Map of Educational Research*. Windsor: NFER Publishing Company.

WATSON, F.R. (1976). *Developments in Mathematics Teaching*. London: Open Books.

Chapter 7
Evaluation and Assessment

No matter how elaborate, impressive or persuasive the arrangements for learning and teaching in a school, they will be of little value unless actually carried out. Head teachers and teachers may extol the organization of their schools and classrooms, but, without means whereby intentions are verified as fulfilling their purpose, the exercise is of little avail. A system to test input/output of schools and classrooms is a necessary feature of curriculum design. Likewise, children need to be checked for learning attainment.

The dispute which has existed for some years in education between the 'traditionalists' and the 'progressives' has given the appearance of relating to different interpretations of curriculum, but underlying the divergence is the contentious issue of 'standards'. Traditionalists' standards are based on past experience of measuring work against expectations, while progressives respect the quality of work and subjectively measure its worth. Either way, standards are the criteria which lie behind patterns of judgement of the quality and value of children's work in schools (Stenhouse 1967 pp. 70-89). Consequently, standards are specifications by which required qualities may be checked, while qualities are degrees of excellence (Choat, 1978, p.121), but the majority of people who condemn present day standards in schools are not referring to this definition. In fact, they are not thinking of standards at all but the basic skills that they consider essential for children to acquire. Basic skills are merely the ability to carry out specific operations in a sequential order by approved methods. Skills require a period of exploration and experimentation by trial and error but, once this stage is overcome, the skill may be performed in its set routine. Standards interpreted in this way are proficiency in the basic skills of reading, writing, and mathematics.

Why, then, the anxiety to return to an emphasis on proficiency in the basic skills? Through being processed in skills, children were able to perform and produce evidence of learning in school by monologuing the printed word, completing pages of writing, and working through pages of sums. Success in these activities was considered as achieving. Irrespective of how the evidence was produced, children had mastered the skills necessary for either further learning or to be placed in suitable jobs. But did the children understand what they were doing when carrying out the skills? They were practised in them so frequently that proficiency was unavoidable. The skill in finding the area of something was to 'multiply length times width', but what is area? 'Turn the divisor upside down and multiply' was the skill needed to divide by fractions, but why is this operation used? Returning to a prerogative of basic skills in mathematics, and sacrificing attention to children as individuals to acquire qualities of excellence through concept acquisition, is retrogressive. If children are to develop in mathematics, they must be allowed a mathematical education and this will not be secured by insisting on basic skills to the detriment of all else.

A return to basic skills will entail a return to formal ways of teaching with mathematics practised as in the days of the eleven plus examination with teachers concentrating on teaching rules and ways of answering sums. This rigid approach to mathematics teaching will encourage a rigid approach to the remainder of the primary school curriculum. By being restricted to their desks to 'do sums', children will be expected to be less active in their pursuit of projects and other experiences that involve inquiry. The primary school curriculum will lose flair and this loss will restrict children in their development as persons with an ability to think, and to be educated for their world. Moreover, the basic skill attitude is ignoring the role of mathematics in the primary school curriculum. If mathematics is everywhere and in almost everything, it is essential that young children should be given the opportunity to partake in a mathematically inspired curriculum and receive a mathematical education which enables them to come to terms with life. Compared to learning rules by rote, as would occur with a return to an emphasis on basic skills, a mathematical education encourages children to enjoy and pursue mathematics, and lead a full and active life by applying their mathematical knowledge in their interests, games, play, ordinary activities of life, etc. Without mathematics, children would not come to terms with their environment, be unable to appreciate its aesthetic qualities, be unaware of its maintenance, protection, and development of society, and be ignorant of its use in their lives and in their future careers. A mathematical education, as stated previously, possesses values which are essential to children as (a) mathematics has practical uses in an individual's activities of life; (b) mathematics is a cultural subject in its own right whereby an individual is led to come to terms with the world in which he lives; (c) mathematics is part of an individual's basic language through which he is able to interpret and communicate with others; and (d) involvement with, and deduction in, mathematics encourages logical and ordered thinking in an individual. These are the spheres within which qualities, and hence standards, should be sought. Basic skills are dismissed and replaced by an attitude that enables children to develop as individuals by proceeding at their pace of learning, and at their level of development, to acquire mathematics at their level of capability.

The 'back to basics brigade' have a short-sighted view of what mathematics is, and its influence on children and the primary school curriculum. No account is taken of the expansion of mathematical content in the primary school. The limitations that a basic skills curriculum has on children are described by Wheatley (1977) when he says:

> There are very many people who talk about a decline in standards in the teaching of mathematics in the primary school. If you were to test today a 'middle of the road' primary school, teaching a mixture of traditional and modern mathematics, it would not do very well on the 1962 Essex test (the eleven-plus examination), and you could say that standards had declined. However, if you tested the same school on the TAMS it would do better. You cannot make assertions about decline in standards at the present time because of the changes in mathematical content of the primary school over the last fifteen years. What everybody has to do is to make up their minds what they would like their eleven year old child's mathematical knowledge to be. Would you like him to be able to do the 1962 test with its emphasis on computation or the TAMS test with its wide variety of mathematical concepts and rich vocabulary? I don't think that there is a choice. The mathematics that the 1962 test examined is an inadequate foundation upon which to develop a child's education.

The impression that most adults have of school, and the 'standards' which they think children should attain, are those that prevailed when they were at school. Little account is taken of scientific, technological and economic developments of recent years, the vast changes in society, recognition of the child as an individual, factors that could impede a child in his learning, the expansion of the **primary school curriculum to enable children to be educated, the** frustrations that have been encountered by primary school teachers, and the pressures imposed on schools from outside for development. Throughout this period of development, the concern of most teachers has been to cope. Very few teachers have had any clear indication of what the new mathematical content involves. Many were thrust into open plan schools without prior experience of teaching in an individualized way, others were forced into new teaching techniques on the whim of a head teacher or some other person merely to 'ride the band-wagon of fashion', while some were lead astray by **misinterpretations of educational jargon. Some blame can be** attached to teachers for allowing these situations to overtake them — every professional should be professionally equipped — and for not acquainting the public sufficiently of the circumstances in schools. Neither can it be denied that there has been inefficiency in some primary schools. Some teachers have remained indifferent to developments in primary education and did not keep abreast of the changing atmosphere by attending in-service courses, seeking further professional training, reading educational journals, books, etc. Other teachers are 'poor' and should not be in classrooms, while a minority have been imbued with an ideal that has been subversive to the educational policy supported by the majority. Meanwhile, until recently, class sizes in most primary schools were large, and in many areas instability of staff was common. With rapid changes of personnel, inexperienced teachers, and many supply teachers to fill gaps, continuity of teaching was lacking.

It was in this climate that the rumblings of declining standards were first heard in the late 1960s, with the publication of the Black Papers. The most pressing concern of the contributors to the Black Papers appears to be the demise of the grammar school. Their main attack centres on the ineffectiveness of comprehensive schools with an anticipated fall in standards, but Black Paper Two (1969) contains articles relating to primary schools. In this edition, Crawford (pp.96-100) claims to present a balanced view but makes a strong case for the retention of the three Rs, Pinn (pp.101-3) is scathing of

Colleges of Education and the training received by student teachers, and teachers who hop on the band-wagon of 'progressive education', and Froome (pp.104-8) alleges 'modern' maths can only be taught by experienced, competent and dedicated teachers who have the mathematical expertise to guide children in their comprehension of concepts. These emotive accounts are supplemented by an article by Bantock (pp.110-8) in which he clarifies misinterpretations of 'discovery methods'. Bantock's is not a reactionary account but an in-depth appraisal of what is meant by 'discovery' and how it affects children's learning. He acknowledges that 'discovery methods' have sought to harness the informal curiosity of children as advocated by Rousseau but maintains that teachers have been confused as to how or when informality should be turned into formality — when 'structure' should be involved and even imposed, and when the demands of the school as an instrument of 'structured' learning should replace the haphazard, if stimulating, early learning experiences. Bantock raises the misguided impressions attributed to Piaget. Piaget, he claims, is not a learning theorist, and it is wrong to think that Piaget's findings in any way validate 'discovery methods'. Piaget implies that concrete actuality is important in children's learning but he does not profess any particular method of presenting it. Bantock adds, 'discovery methods' constitute an important but limited addition to the vocabulary of teaching. They are useful for arousing interest, as motivators, and for introducing children to possibilities beyond those of formal methods, but enthusiasm needs to be curbed by a thorough and careful understanding by teachers as to what they are aiming to accomplish.

Bennett's (1976) findings of the effects of different teaching organizations on primary school children's attainment added impetus to criticisms of standards. After verifying that teachers were teaching according to the styles professed, Bennett selected ten year old children in the classes of thirteen informal, twelve mixed, and twelve formal teachers. The children were tested for attainment in reading, mathematics, and English before entering their fourth year class, and retested in the following June. The tests were chosen so that they would not be biased to any particular mode of teaching, but (p.154) only one third of the teachers felt there was no bias, one sixth that the tests were biased towards informal teaching, and the remaining half that there was some degree of bias towards formal teaching. The results in reading provided clear evidence for the better performance of formal and mixed pupils in reading progress (p.88).

The effect was more apparent among boys, but there was evidence to suggest that low achieving boys in formal classes performed less well than those of equivalent achievement in mixed and informal classes. In mathematics, better progress in mathematical understanding was evident with formal teaching styles, with the exception of the lowest achieving boys (p.93). Whether understanding in Bennett's view referred to instrumental or relational understanding is not specified. Overall, pupils in formal classes showed significantly better progress in English than those in mixed and informal classes (p.96). Mixed pupils also showed significantly better progress than informal pupils.

These findings appear conclusive when studied with the diagrams in the book, but a disconcerting anomaly appears when the research material is studied closely. Appendix Table C.1 (p.177) does not comply with the diagrams as this shows mean gains for the respective groups as follows:

	Reading	*Mathematics*	*English*
Formal	5.9	6.3	5.9
Mixed	7.6	2.8	9.2
Informal	3.9	4.6	4.8

This evidence suggests that the mixed organizations made the most substantial gains in reading and English, and is contrary to what Bennett claims.

Bennett's research design is suspect as no indication is given of the capabilities of children in the respective groups, the socio-economic factors related to the schools, the length of time each class had experienced a particular teaching organization, and the experience of the teachers, while the method of testing is open to criticism. Nothing is mentioned about the children themselves and their general performance. There is a likelihood that some children were under-performing and, when tested, gave evidence of their true capability. If these children belonged to the formal group, the results were spurious. Also, the number of children in some groups is very small and this does not abide with valid research. Socio-economic class is generally accepted as the most accurate means of prediction of success or failure in schools, and, in recent years, much attention has been given to the education of disadvantaged children. A researcher has a responsibility to demonstrate the reliability of his method of testing and to show that specific variables do not influence results, but Bennett does not do this. Consequently, Bennett may have measured the effect of socio-economic class or differing learning potential rather than teaching styles (Rogers and Barron 1976).

Neither is any indication given of how long each class had been subjected to the particular organization. The children in the informal classes may have been new to the experience and were catching up on activities which they had missed when taught formally. As fifty per cent of the teachers considered the tests favoured formal teaching, the experience and attitude of the teachers are fundamental issues for consideration. Formal teachers are usually older and more experienced than informal teachers. They place a greater emphasis on children's acquisition of basic skills in reading, writing, and mathematics with constant practice and repetition in what they consider to be necessary for children to learn. There are also limited opportunities for children to develop in aspects other than the basic skills. Resultantly, Bennett may have been testing teacher experience and attitude rather than teaching organizations. Moreover, Bennett's data indicate the contention made previously that the eleven-plus examination influences performance in the three Rs. Five formal classes but only three informal classes were liable for the examination so a possibility existed that this variable influenced children's performances. The use of standardized tests in mathematics is questionable. Such tests provide evidence of instrumental understanding, i.e. whether children are able to obtain correct answers. They do not check relational understanding. Although Bennett's research created much fervour, the conclusions should not be taken for granted; particularly when the class which achieved better than any other class was an 'informal' class.

Similarly, the results of a 'basic test in numeracy', given by the Institute of Mathematics and 'Its Applications' in November, 1977, to more than eight thousand pupils in their last year of compulsory education (fifth year pupils), was given widespread publicity, and used as a weapon to condemn mathematics teaching in schools. 'The most basic skills' were tested, but the report Clarke (1978) must be scrutinized more thoroughly than just taking the results at face value. Six local education authorities were chosen to cover different parts of England and Wales, and each authority was asked to nominate up to ten schools that would provide a cross-section of the children in its area. No indication was given of which schools were chosen, or the pupils who comprised the sample. A possibility existed, that the sample could have been selected from the lowest streams in the schools. As with Bennett *(op. cit.)*, no attention was given to socio-economic factors, teacher experience, teacher attitudes, and measured performance of the pupils against general performance.

The test may have been thought a joke by some fifteen year olds, and completed with fallacious answers. Disregarding the weaknesses in research design, the Institute report presents an interesting exercise. Certain questions in the test are similar to those used by Ward (1979) and Sumner (1975) both of whom conducted investigations in mathematics with ten and eleven year old primary school children. Ward had a sample of almost 2,300 children and used four different but parallel versions of test papers, while Sumner had a much smaller sample.

The questions used by the latter and which resembled those of Clarke *(op. cit.)* were:

A   Ward (7)   392 x 7   Clarke (3b) 6 x 79
            (8)   283 x 7

B   (9)   255 ÷ 6   (4b) 243 ÷ 9
            (10)   315 ÷ 6

C   Ward (11)   How much is left from £2 after buying 4 books costing 30p each?

            (12)   How much is left from £2 after buying 5 books costing 25p each?

Clarke (13)

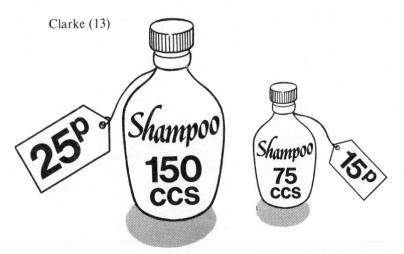

How much do I save if I buy 2 large bottles of shampoo instead of taking the same quantity in small bottles?

Ward (13)

0	6	2	9	9

D

What is the next number this meter will show? Write it in here.

Ward (14)   The mileometer on a car shows

0	2	6	9	9
   miles

What will it show after the car has gone one more mile?

Clarke (12)   A cheque is made out for one hundred and forty nine pounds and nine pence.
Write this amount in figures.

E   Ward (74)   This chart shows how a class of 40 children get to school. About how many of these children walk to school?

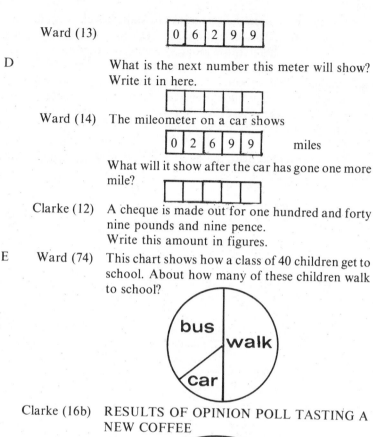

Clarke (16b)   RESULTS OF OPINION POLL TASTING A NEW COFFEE

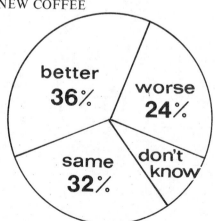

If 250 people were consulted altogether, how many thought the quality of the coffee was just the same as before?

F   Sumner(Ii)   Which is the latest train I could take from Reading to be in Bath by 2 o'clock in the afternoon.

Paddington	06 15	07 50	09 45	10 45	11 45	12 45
Reading	06 55	08 24	10 19		12 19	
Swindon	07 38	09 08	10 54	11 19	13 04	13 19
Bath	08 14	09 44	11 29	12 18	13 42	14 22
Bristol	08 30	10 00	11 45	12 35	14 00	14 40

Clarke (17)   If I cannot leave Camtown until 3 p.m. what is the earliest I can be in Manchester?

CAMTOWN	0712	0910	1312	1621	1907
BELFORD	—	0941	1342	1652	1937
GREEN MILL	0845	1055	—	1806	2020
MANCHESTER	1023	1234	1602	1953	2200

The percentages of wrong and not attempted answers to these questions were:

Clarke – Institute of Mathematics

	Bucks		Dyfed		Essex		Leeds		ILEA		Cl'land		Ward/ Sumner		
	B	G	B	G	B	G	B	G	B	G	B	G	B	G	
A	15	13	16	14	21	15	21	18	24	26	31	22	50	44	(7)
													49	42	(8)
B	14	14	19	18	26	20	22	19	31	30	32	26	59	54	(9)
													56	44	(10)
C	19	26	25	31	23	24	26	31	33	43	40	35	33	38	(11)
													38	40	(12)
D	19	21	29	33	34	35	35	44	53	54	55	49	53	66	(13)
													46	58	(14)
E	38	45	46	58	44	48	49	64	58	72	68	69	25	24	(74)
F	36	41	53	61	40	46	47	61	58	70	69	69	60(B&G)		(Ii)

B (Boys)   G (Girls)

After contemplation, E was considered invalid. Although both questions require deductions from pie graphs, the primary school answer is a fraction and the secondary school a percentage. The questions in A and B involve operations of multiplication and division respectively. Whereas the secondary school pupils were required to operate on a two figure number, the primary school children operated on a three figure number with multiplication. Allowing for this extra degree of difficulty, the primary school children's performance is not markedly different. The secondary school pupils were assisted by a diagram in C, but there is some rationalization with the question. Overall, the primary school children fared equally as well with their two questions. Question D for both groups requires straightforward numeration for the answers. Once more, the primary school children performed with credit compared to the fifth formers. The requirement from both groups for the railway time-tables (F) is identical, and, in some instances, the primary school children did better than the secondary school pupils.

Schools should be providing children with an education that will equip them to become responsible members of society, but to do this schools must adhere to the wishes of society. In turn, society must ask itself whether it wishes its children to be educated as capable human beings, or whether it wishes its children to become automated individuals without the capability to think. If the former is desired qualities of excellence are the criteria but, if the latter is accepted, 'standards' are the mode. The majority of the population would wish for the former and they must not be swayed by a vociferous minority who either distort or do not comprehend the true situation. The choice of qualities of excellence places a great responsibility on teachers. They must ensure that they are equipped to fulfil the role which society has entrusted to them. When pressures from society are on them and when they are being asked to account for their endeavours, teachers must respond by demonstrating the worth of the education being provided.

This prerogative emphasises the need for clear and unbiased thought when evaluating the curriculum. In some schools, no valid evaluation measures are applied with the result that the teachers adopt indifferent attitudes to their teaching. In other schools, a head teacher with a fetish for examinations, diagnostic tests, intelligence tests, verbal reasoning tests, etc. (so that the teachers are constantly testing to the exclusion of productive teaching) may think that he is evaluating the curriculum, but these procedures are assessments of children and not evaluation. These examples show the confusion that exists in schools between evaluation and assessment, but not only in schools are the terms and their functions confused. Glenn (1977 pp.73-84) refers to the 'assessment of objective' and later (p.97) comments on 'a planned test of objectives'.

Confusion may exist between assessment and evaluation with the terms used indiscriminately and interchangeably, but the distinction has a subtle bearing on what is measured, and to whom it refers. As MacDonald (1976 pp.87-91) explains, assessment makes statements about the recipients of an educational service; statements about their actual and potential accomplishments in relation to the opportunities for learning provided by that service. Assessment is the basis for decisions of what children will receive in further provision and predictions of their future accomplishments. On the other hand, evaluation does not make statements about recipients but about the educational service. Evaluation statements serve decisions about educational provisions.

Evaluation, is a measurement of teaching input/output, and suggests the existence of recognisable objectives about which achievement or non-achievement can be determined. In turn, the selection of objectives demands a judgement of what a school can hope to achieve (Wiseman and Pidgeon, 1970, pp.22-4). The curriculum should be an efficient instrument that through evaluation determines the means to the end. Evaluation of the means is a hard and fast appraisal of a school's attempt to implement its curriculum, and as such is an evaluation of the school. The school is judged for its effectiveness by questioning whether children have opportunities for equality and are being presented with teaching which is productive by bringing about learning.

Kerr (1968) summarises this contention when he states that in curriculum design the objectives should be the first component identified. The teacher will then know what she is striving towards, and be able to decide 'what' or 'how' to employ her teaching methods and organization. Evaluation of objectives should produce evidence about the nature, direction, and extent of changes which have taken place with children's educational endeavours. A school should have certain cognitive achievements, attitudes, values and interests that it is encouraging its pupils to acquire, and these are obtained only by providing appropriate learning experiences. Throughout teaching, it is necessary to make constant judgements of objectives, organizations, content and methods.

Realistic objectives are essential if account is to be taken of the individuality of children within a school. Objectives are successfully evaluated only when each child is considered as an individual. Children vary in their ability, growth, personality, interests, home background, etc., and curriculum objectives, and hence educational objectives, should be related closely to each child's needs. Objectives that refer to a whole class of children are pointless, and objectives which cannot be achieved by a child are useless.

As stated previously, the objectives of mathematical education are twofold — (a) preparing those children who will become mathematicians and eventually apply their specialized knowledge in industry, commerce, management, and teaching, and (b) preparing the other children to a degree of competence in mathematics for use and pleasure in their ordinary lives. The extent of children's aspirations in either direction is dependent upon the psychological factors of intelligence and the ability to abstract, but the level of teaching and the degree of learning are influenced by the teacher's awareness of how children acquire mathematics, aspects likely to retard mathematical development, features related to mathematical progression, and presentation of learning. Above all, a teacher has a responsibility to ensure that the children in her class are attaining in mathematics. This will not emerge unless she abides by the principles of the teaching of mathematics enumerated in the previous chapter.

Expectations from children are taken to the classroom or are quickly acquired by a teacher. Irrespective of whether she has a child-centre or knowledge-centred philosophy, teacher expectations revolve around the stimulation offered that, in turn, engenders a self-fulfilling prophecy in children. Translated into classroom terms, goals are specified of what is wanted from the children. There will be many areas of mathematics within the teacher's goals if the children are to receive a sound mathematical education. These should be encouraged with interesting activities and experiences, and promoted in ways that will arouse motivation instead of being prescribed, dull exercises which follow a set pattern. A teacher must be aware of possible areas of progression when a child reaches a specific stage in his mathematics and provide suitable experiences to enable the progression.

The cry heard from some primary school teachers is, 'tell me how to teach mathematics'. Apart from catering for progression and bearing in mind children's levels of development and pace of learning, a teacher should promote a climate in which she is warm, accepting and sensitive that encourages reciprocity between her pupils and herself. It is implicit that the teacher institutes a system of teacher-pupil relationships that promote learning. Children's capabilities should not be under-estimated as they are capable of achieving in mathematics when given stimulation. Mathematical knowledge should not be assumed but each level of mathematical development determined.

Evaluation should signify whether organization and method are satisfactory and whether they are suitable to mathematical learning. The initial consideration is the overall planning and organization. If the teaching approach is specialization, the teacher will need to consider whether the children are using mathematics capably in other areas of curriculum content. She should reason also whether sufficient time is allocated to the teaching of mathematics. This is particularly pertinent if an integrated day is followed. An integrated day does not necessarily imply an integration of content. In fact, in most integrated days, separation of reading, writing and mathematics is practised, but a teacher must ensure that sufficient time is being spent on them. If integration of content is favoured, it is necessary to ascertain that children are developing in mathematics at their degree of ability and not being allowed to rely on existing knowledge. Should evaluation reveal that the children are not progressing, steps should be taken to remedy the situation. Either special arrangements should be made for the children or the organization changed.

Specialization may be taken to an extreme with one teacher specializing in mathematics throughout a school. This is a sad state of affairs in a primary school. It is imperative for mathematics to be taken by the class teacher if she is to note its use by children in other areas of the curriculum and ensure that they are using it at their level of development. The compromise is for a teacher to have special responsibility for mathematics and act as advisor to her colleagues.

Assuming that the class teacher has responsibility for mathematics and specialization is the approach, irrespective of a fixed time-table or an integrated day, the teacher must decide her organization for the acquisition of classroom goals. Emphasis has been placed on children as individuals throughout this book. This can be taken too literally to imply that each child must be engaged in separate work. Such is too complicated for the probationary teacher to organize and is beyond the capability of many experienced teachers. The child as an individual suggests that he is recognized and treated as an individual with the teacher conversant of his level of development and pace of learning. A teacher must ascertain these factors before productive learning is possible. This she may do by concept checks, tests, or by taking the children through elementary stages of mathematical notions to decipher how the children cope with them. A child's performance is communicated to the teacher through observation and association. Checking and testing are useful when doubt exists. Having assessed the children individually, the teacher may then decide to group various children according to achievement levels but, whatever happens in a group, each child's performance must be recognized. Some children may not achieve at the prescribed level, and this will entail making provisions on an individual basis or reallocation to another group. Other children may progress beyond the level of other members of their group. Such children should not be held back by being given experiences that are repetitive and boring but be reassigned to another group or catered for individually. Some children will be engaged in tasks which are individual to themselves and frequently these children will be those who are under-achieving or who are displaying outstanding ability in mathematics. Providing individually for these children should be within the capability of a primary school teacher if she has organized her remaining group work efficiently. On occasions, some mathematics for whole class participation may be decided upon, but, after the initial activity and experience, the class will split in different directions according to their levels of development, and again the teacher will have to group. The essence of a teacher's organization is flexibility for children to be allocated to activities and experiences suitable to them, while she must consider how association is to be effective.

Children using a set text book, series of work cards, or work book is followed in some schools but such a system is not condoned. This is fitting children to mathematics and individuality is lost. Organization is at a minimum. The only requirement is for each child to have a book and work on the appropriate page. There is a temptation with such an organization for a teacher to rely on the book as the teaching medium. Children need interpretation and guidance from a teacher no matter the teaching technique, and many exercises in books, work cards or work books need prior activities and teaching before the listed work can be understood. If this form of teaching applies, the teacher must still decide how it is to be organized.

Evaluation will reveal the success or otherwise of a teacher's basic classroom organization. Certain elementary yet fundamental issues will be scrutinized. The teacher should consider whether sufficient planning of activities is possible within her chosen organization. A mixed ability class necessitates provisions for more groups to be organized than a streamed class. Account should be taken of whether the children have comfortable places in which to work. Concern must be given that materials are accessible when needed — structural apparatus, mathematical tools such as rulers, compasses, protractors, set squares, tape measures, clinometer, etc., various forms of paper, exercise books, pencils (sharpened), coloured crayons, relevant text books, work cards, or work books, and materials that may be in the possession of another teacher. The teacher must institute a system for when children have completed their current task or when her attention is required. These aspects are sometimes overlooked by teachers and are the cause of an organized classroom becoming disorganized. Above all, the teacher must systematize how she is to organize to allow time for association with those children who need it, and when she is to teach. A teacher cannot be expected to deal with several children at the same time. She must evolve a routine that enables her to spend time with children individually.

A teacher can concentrate on method when the organizational considerations are resolved. Teaching method was discussed in the previous chapter, and the contention made that it required thought. Certain evaluation issues will inevitably accrue. Does a particular method relate to instrumental understanding or relational understanding? To what extent is play necessary as the teaching method with various mathematical notions? Are the surrounding neighbourhood and other aspects of environment being used profitably as teaching method? Is a particular form of educational technology the correct approach for a context of learning? Has a large collection of text books, word cards, and work books been obtained, and are they being used according to each child's stage of progression? Have alternative approaches to learning been considered, e.g. when a child has not conceptualized, is the same approach with the same apparatus repeated or are other methods attempted? Are the children required to record everything in the same way? Do the children pursue and enjoy their work with the method? Are the activities and experiences meeting the children's needs? Have provisions been made for feedback from children? Is the method sufficiently challenging to the children? Is the method appropriate to the child's level of development and pace of learning?

Within the organization and method, the teacher will fit the content to be learned. Numerous references could be quoted that list mathematical content thought suitable for primary school children to acquire. The emphasis within this book has been for a teacher to possess a framework of mathematics but this framework should not be bestowed on children. Instead, the teacher should concentrate on the values which the acquisition of mathematics will bring to children. As such, the teacher should strive for qualities of excellence in mathematics. This dispenses with a common curriculum in mathematics; particularly a curriculum that stipulates learning skills by specified ages. Children's varied mathematical abilities should be taken into account, and a teacher should be aware that progression in mathematics is not linear. The teacher should select activities and experiences relevant to each child from her framework of mathematics. To assist her, she should devise a basis of desired outcomes for children that are partially ordered and allow for flexibility in progression, while bearing in mind that higher order concepts cannot be acquired prior to foundation concepts. With this approach, children should develop in mathematics. This development is broad with each mathematical notion providing understanding for related notions. It could be said that mathematical content has no bounds, its evaluation being answers to 'why' a notion is taught, 'how' it is taught, and 'what' are the best forms of teaching method and organization for certain children. Evaluation does not measure individual children's acquisition of mathematics; this is the role of assessment.

The results of evaluation should indicate if any of the teaching arrangements may be improved. Much evaluation arises from value analysis. Irrespective of formal or informal teaching, a teacher should subjectively appraise her teaching and consider ways of improving it. No teacher should be complacent and satisfied with her teaching. She should constantly explore new and better ways of teaching. A teacher who has ceased to rationalize her own teaching has ceased to teach.

Evaluation of the means used to secure objectives should be a continuous process and this will necessitate keeping teachers' records and profiles of children's achievements. The profiles will show the progress or otherwise that children are making, and the success or failure of the means. If there are signs of a lack of progression, the indication is the means are failing and need be revised. The records will show what the teacher has attempted to teach and these can be compared with achievement profiles to establish whether the teaching has been profitable. Although some teachers will devise schemes of their own that break-down objectives into specified goals, the recording system is the head teacher's prerogative. To institute an effective method of recording is not easy as there is a danger of over-recording with every single item accounted for. This causes teachers to become imbued with administrative details that are either ignored, or, if followed implicitly, are a hinderance to classroom activites. The justification for whom, why and what particular records are kept should be resolved. The extent of the records' uses and their effectiveness are a major concern. Through records, a head teacher should determine whether his teachers are proceeding towards the school's objectives, and the teachers judge whether the means are attaining the ends.

A balanced recording procedure that is acted upon for its evaluative function will eliminate misguided impressions of evaluation and assessment. Children's achievement profiles will, through assessment, make statements about their learning accomplishments and refer to each individually. Only when a consensus of the achievements is made are the profiles a component of the evaluation process. It is not the achievement profiles but the information which they give when correlated with the teachers' records that act as the evaluation mechanism.

The assessment of children has not been fashionable in recent years. 'Progressive' education has considered assessment to be socially and educationally undesirable as competition is encouraged through grading children's achievements. Advocates of this premise favour abandoning streamed classes for mixed ability classes, but, even in the latter, children must be assessed if learning appropriate to their levels of development is to be given. Consequently, three categories of assessment can be identified — normative, criterial, and diagnostic. Normative assessment compares each child with a norm. This type of assessment is made by those demanding standards in mathematics; although the norms are based on what it is felt children should acquire instead of a standardized norm. Critical assessment decides whether a child has reached a criterion set by a teacher; an assessment of pupil outcome measured by teacher expectations. A child could be achieving poorly if compared to other children on a normative assessment but achieving according to his level of development on a critical assessment. Diagnostic assessment differs from the two previous types of assessment as its purpose is to discover the nature of a learner's difficulties. Once the deficiency is detected by diagnosis, a child can be given the appropriate activities and experiences that will allow formation of the relevant concept, or practice in the particular skill.

It is imperative that a valid form of assessment is instituted in a school, and that the assessment procedures assess what they are meant to assess. Assessment in mathematics, according to the ILEA Mathematics Inspectorate (1978 pp.1-3), should be measuring the acquisition of concepts, knowledge of facts, performance of skills, and application to problems. Much of this assessment will be carried out informally by a teacher during association with children, and when work is marked. Through reciprocity, the teacher will judge how a child is responding to certain learning, and feedback to the teacher will indicate the child's comprehension. Nevertheless, teachers have a right to expect ways of defining each child's level of development apart from relying on their own judgements. They need re-assurance on occasions of the levels of understanding shown by children even though they may be aware of them by instinct and experience. Children have scant information about their progress if no means of assessment is operated. Assessment resolves into feedback for the children. They are informed of wrong conclusions, incorrect applications, poor attitudes, and the degree of concep- tualization or level of skill to be reached. Feedback is motivational for some children whereas for others it may discourage, but it indicates to either group their attainment of goals which they have set themselves, and the extent to which they are meeting teacher expectations.

Apart from reciprocity, a teacher and children need other forms of assessment that may be implemented formally, but care should be taken that the mechanism is fulfilling the role of assessment and is not a curriculum component. Examinations are used often as normative assessment but this is incorrect. The eleven-plus examination for example is an objective when children are prepared to pass it. An objective cannot assess itself. The examination merely defines those children who either pass or fail. Its function is a yardstick to specify the capabilities of each child at the time he sat the examination. Neither is the examination a means of evaluation as it does not indicate whether the correct means to pass have been carried out in the school. Even if inadequate means are used, some capable children may still pass. Some educationalists may argue that this could not have been the case as inadequate means would result in a high rate of failure and to pass is evidence that the necessary means were employed. Such an argument does not consider those children who had the necessary capability to pass but who failed. An evaluation of the means to specify whether each child was doing justice or otherwise to himself is a better indicator. A school may claim that it had x number of passes but x plus y may be the correct amount if alternative means were adopted. Neither is the 'not so able' child considered when examinations are used as judgements. The critical assessment of whether these children have achieved to their level of capability is not considered. The effort, interests and values of those below the qualification bar are ignored by examinations if the children do not meet the prescribed levels to sit the examinations.

Tests may act either as normative or critical assessment to measure learning as they indicate children's individual performances, but are unreliable if factors likely to inhibit learning are not taken into account. Tests are sets of oral or written questions designed to test specific learning according to children's levels of development. This contrasts with examinations which, although consisting of questions, make no distinction of achievement levels.

Testing takes place in classrooms at an informal level. Teachers constantly seek whether children have learned particular things. Testing often occurs during association when teachers ask for oral responses to gauge whether learning has been acquired. Children's written work is looked at by teachers to ensure that they are able to complete a task.

Formal testing may be undertaken in a number of ways, but a common practice is for a teacher to devise her own test. For example, when children are involved in learning tables of multiplication, the teacher will often devise a 'table test' to measure the extent of learning. This is known as a 'short answer test' or 'completion test' when the predetermined answer to a question is completed by recall. Other forms of test which may be used are 'multiple choice' when the correct response from usually four or five options is required, 'true or false' when the testee has to decide on a given statement, 'matching' when a list of items and a list of responses are given to pair, and 'ordering' when a series of statements are given for the pupil to arrange.

What do these tests prove? They merely indicate whether a child has learned the particular knowledge or skill being tested, and, even then, a degree of chance exists when selecting a correct answer, particularly with a 'true or false' test with its 50% degree of probability. A child is tested within the confines of the test and not to the extent that he applies his level of understanding to discover patterns of relationship. The assumption behind such tests is that children are measured according to a predetermined criteria. The tests are used as critical assessments when either the head teacher or the teacher compiles a test to ascertain whether certain required data has been learned (as with the 'table test') but normative use is restricted to the particular school. A head teacher may compare the extent of learning of his year groups from year to year by using the same test, but this gives no indication of the children's performances compared to other schools. Moreover, the adoption of this practice is more evaluation than assessment as appraisal of a class as a whole is being undertaken, and the teacher's endeavours evaluated, instead of each child's progress being assessed.

A head teacher should use a 'standardised test' to critically analyse the children on a normative basis. 'Standardized tests' are constructed by experts, and standardized on a representative sample of the population. They operate normatively on the assumption of being common to all children but this is not so if children have been learning mathematical notions which differ from those in the standardized test. The test, should be used only when it is suitable for assessing what is required to be assessed. Child (1973, pp. 253-4) categorizes two forms of standardized tests — ability tests and attainment tests. Ability tests attempt to measure the all-round mental efficiency of a person without necessarily indicating specific subject skills. Verbal and non-verbal reasoning tests are examples of such tests. Attainment tests correlate to some extent with ability tests but are designed to sample achievement in specific subjects and to enable a reasonably accurate estimate of attainment. Attainment tests operate on the principle that common objectives prevail in mathematics with each test appropriate for children of specific ages but, apart from the possibility of testing what has not been learned, the tests cannot reveal the degree that understanding has been acquired.

Standardized tests do not provide diagnostic information. If valid assessments of children's levels of development are required, 'diagnostic tests' and 'concepts checks' must be the means. 'Diagnostic tests are devised to systematically break-down stages of an operation or a skill to detect the point where the individual is failing to cope with the task. They may identify an underlying problem and enable treatment to be given to overcome the difficulty but this does not ensure that understanding has been achieved. As stages are diagnosed, the treatment may consist of learning a set routine and this could be possible through rote learning. The only means whereby understanding in mathematics can be certified is through checking for conservation. 'Concept checks', are not tests. A child's ability to hold an attribute constant in the face of change is termed conservation. According to Piaget (1952 pp.3-5), every notion, whether it is scientific or a matter of common sense, presupposes a set of principles of conservation. A classical example of conservation of quantity is Piaget's check with continuous quantities when liquid from one of two identical beakers is poured into another beaker of different dimensions. Children are said to conserve if they assert that the amounts of liquid are the same despite the change of appearance.

Through observations of children with various activities, an alert teacher possesses knowledge of the concepts acquired by each child, but doubt arises frequently in a classroom and the easiest way to overcome the doubt is to implement a concept check. To assist in the task, the teacher may consult the Nuffield 'Checking Up' Guides or the ILEA Mathematics Inspectorate's (*op. cit.*) 'Checkpoints' but, as the latter (p.2) states, it is not easy checking whether a concept has been acquired. Complete precision in concept assessment may be difficult to ascertain, but that does not justify abandoning the task. Concepts are the means of children understanding mathematics and, although factual knowledge and skills may be learned independently of concepts by relying on memory, the relevant factual knowledge and skills cannot be applied in a problem unless the required concepts are formed. When memory fails, there is no way of thinking out problems from first principles unless the concepts have been formed (ILEA Mathematics Inspectorate *op. cit.*).

Children's achievement profiles in mathematics should concentrate on concept acquisition. As mentioned previously, a teacher's records will indicate the experiences given to children, but the children's achievement profiles will specify what each child has acquired. The construction of achievement profiles should be an essential item in a school. The ILEA Mathematics Inspectorate (*op. cit.* p.24) suggest that an agreed list should be established by staff discussion with each concept, piece of factual knowledge, skill and application expressed in a way that describes what the child understands, knows, or is able to do. For example, rather than 'symmetry' a teacher may write 'Can recognize and construct shapes and designs with one line of symmetry, two or more lines of symmetry, and rotational symmetry'.

The way children are assessed in mathematics indicates a school's objectives if achievements are used to evaluate teaching. How teaching has been approached, and the methods used are signified. A rigid approach with an emphasis on basic skills and factual knowledge indicates testing as the prerogative. A flexible approach indicates that understanding is monitored by concept checks. Irrespective of whether teaching is formal or informal, assessment of children and evaluation of the curriculum provide a teacher with the mechanism to appraise her teaching and consider ways of improving it. In fact, no teacher should be satisfied with her teaching, and complacent with the techniques which she uses. She should constantly explore how her efforts could be improved. A teacher who has ceased to consider her own teaching has ceased to teach. Evaluation and assessment should be continuous processes with the teacher questioning how she wishes her pupils to acquire mathematics — by either relational understanding or merely being able to carry out the motions.

Education is the means of preparing a child to make his future contribution to society, and this can be paralleled to either sight-seeing or social travel. When sight-seeing, the tourist sees the surface aspects of a culture only, but in social travel the investigator purposefully explores the way of living to understand the people and their problems. Schools that ignore assessment and evaluation are only sight-seeing. They have no wish to verify whether their pupils are attaining qualities of excellence. When assessment and evaluation operate, the education of each child is rationalized. Children become aware that qualities of excellence are to be achieved, and that the teacher has a degree of expectation which she seeks to maintain.

REFERENCES

BANTOCK, G.H. (1969). 'Discovery Methods'. In: COX, C.B. and DYSON, A.E. (Eds). *Black Paper Two*. London: Critical Quarterly.

BENNETT, N. (1976). *Teaching Styles and Pupil Progress*. London: Open Books.

CHILD, D. (1973). *Psychology and the Teacher*. London: Holt, Rinehart & Winston.

CHOAT, E. (1978). *Children's Acquisition of Mathematics*. Windsor: NFER Publishing Company.

CLARKE, N. (1978). *A Pilot Test of Basic Numeracy of Fourth and Fifth-Year Secondary School Pupils*. Southend: The Institute of Mathematics and Its Applications.

CRAWFORD, G.W.J. (1969). 'The Primary School: A Balanced View'. In COX, C.B. and DYSON, A.E. (Eds). *Black Paper Two*. London: Critical Quarterly.

FROOME, S.H. (1969). 'The Mystique of Modern Maths'. In COX, C.B. and DYSON, A.E. (Eds). *Black Paper Two*. London: Critical Quarterly.

GLENN, J.A. (Ed) (1977). *Teaching Primary Mathematics*. London: Harper & Row.

ILEA Mathematics Inspectorate (1978). *Primary School Mathematics 2 Checkpoints*. London: ILEA.

KERR, J.F. (1968). 'The Problem of Curriculum Reform'. In: KERR, J.F. (Ed) *Changing the Curriculum*. London: University of London Press.

MACDONALD, B. (1976). 'Who's Afraid of Evaluation', *Education* 3-13, **4**, 2, 87-91.

PIAGET, J. (1952). *The Child's Conception of Number*. London: Routledge & Kegan Paul.

PINN, D.M. (1969). 'What Kind of Primary School?' In: COX, C.B. and DYSON, A.E. (Eds) *Black Paper Two*. London: Critical Quarterly.

ROGERS, V.R. and BARRON, J. (1976, 30 April). 'Questioning the Evidence', *The Times Educational Supplement*.

STENHOUSE, L. (1967). *Culture and Education*. London: Nelson.

SUMNER, R. (1975). *Tests of Attainment in Mathematics in Schools*. Windsor: NFER Publishing Company.

WARD, M. (1979). *Mathematics and the ten year old*. London: Evans Methuen.

WHEATLEY, D. (1977). 'Mathematical Concepts and Language 1937-1977', *The New Era*, **58**, 5, 134-7.

WISEMAN, S. and PIDGEON, D. (1970). *Curriculum Evaluation*. Windsor: NFER Publishing Company.

Chapter 8
The Expanding Landscape

'Maths teachers must try harder' was the headline of an article in a national newspaper (Rowlands 1979). Alleging that records kept since 1967 had shown a progressive deterioration in 'standards', the article contended that a report prepared by the Association of British Chambers of Commerce was pressing for urgent action to improve 'numeracy' in schools. The Association wanted a minimum number of hours devoted to teaching mathematics in primary schools, and stated that unqualified teachers should not be allowed to teach the subject. An investigation was called for to see 'whether "modern" mathematics is a satisfactory "method" of teaching pupils the arithmetic needed for work'.

The authenticity of this document and the biased reporting are open to criticism. The article was slanted to condemn present practice in schools, and geared to be sensational. It would be interesting to see what records were kept, and to know how deterioration had been ascertained. Were valid research procedures followed to justify the claims? 'Action to improve numeracy' indicates an intention of achieving arithmetical proficiency regardless of improving mathematical competence and the development of children as lively, thinking persons. 'Modern' maths was taken out of context, and to allege that the subject is taught by unqualified teachers is false. Unqualified teachers have not been allowed to teach in primary schools for some years. The Association would more likely find unqualified teachers in private schools, and these teachers would be performing as the Association wishes by concentrating on 'number basics'.

This report is another example of the way primary schools and the teaching of mathematics are attacked without considering the factors that surround them. The attitude prompts a response such as wearing the slogan 'teaching primary mathematics is more difficult than many outside primary schools imagine' around the neck of every primary school child for all to see.

Concern is not given by the dissenters to the importance of mathematics in children's lives, and its influence on the primary school curriculum. Theirs is a short-sighted view that sees arithmetic as a tool of convenience. The attitude does not differ from that of 1870 when state education was geared to the sons and daughters of the working class. Times and society have changed. There is greater enlightenment of what children should receive from education. Instead of continually condemning teachers and 'standards' in primary schools, efforts should be made towards cooperation. How many of the dissenters have been into a primary school classroom to see what is being attempted? How many have taken the trouble to read any literature on the principles being followed in education? As this book has indicated, there are many things which could be improved in primary education, but this will not be achieved by constantly antagonizing the teachers. The issue must be examined objectively, and those outside education should not be led astray by the biased interests of minorities whether it be industry, commerce or journalism. Effort should be made for children to enjoy, and take an interest in, their education. It does not take long for enthusiasm to disappear, and this could happen to Jane, the child quoted in earlier chapters.

My most recent contact with Jane was by telephone. Amid excitement of explaining an impending school visit, she interjected to say that she was learning the multiplication tables of 'two' and 'three'.

'How are you getting on?' I inquired.

'Not very well', she answered.

'Why not?'

'I can't remember them'

'You can't remember them. Have you used blocks to help you?'

'No, we haven't any blocks like you've got', she replied.

'Next time you come, we'll do tables with the blocks,' I suggested.

'Oh, good. I'll like that.'

Jane has steadily pursued her indoctrination in arithmetic. How this contrasts with an incident on a previous visit. During washing up after lunch, she noticed a china funnel. Her inquisitiveness needed satisfying, and she spent several minutes experimenting with the flow of water through the funnel. This was a new experience for Jane, and sadly reflected a loss of water play at school and at home.

Young children are inquisitive and active beings. They are eager to satisfy their curiosity, prepared to inquire, willing to create, and anxious to please. No task is beyond them in their play and other activities. They attempt to explore, manipulate, and control the elements that they encounter. But what has happened to many of them by the time they complete their compulsory education? Some pupils are only too anxious to leave school; education has been just a passing phase in their lives.

Realization of this was brought home forcibly by a group of junior school teachers who had spent time observing mathematics and children in Nursery and Infants' School classrooms. These teachers were taken aback by the attitudes of the children and the wealth of mathematics in the classrooms. Their concern was the limited development made by children by the time they leave primary school.

Why does the potential displayed in the early years evaporate? Is sufficient being done in primary schools to sustain the potential? If not, why does this state of affairs exist? If there is a decline in achievement, who is responsible?

It is easy to blame teachers, but causes of deterioration and lack of aspiration as children get older are not easily defined. Teachers are the agents of society with a bestowed authority to fulfil their function in the way they believe is expected of them. Society must shoulder some blame for not encouraging its young to develop as responsible, capable human beings. Nevertheless, it is to schools that society looks for solutions.

Remedies will not be found by adopting a common curriculum with imposed 'standards'. This will revert to former times with children drained of enthusiasm by boring, repetitive sequences. Young children's enthusiasm must not be allowed to dissipate in the primary school but be harnessed to develop their capabilities by seeing, appreciating and making use of the world in which they live. Children have an ever-widening horizon. Their development is through contact with an expanding landscape. Growing up is experiencing wider horizons acquired from home, neighbourhood, visits, play, games, etc., and understanding this expanding landscape depends upon the capability to read patterns of relationship within it. Mathematics is the key to this understanding. It is the means of providing the relationships, concepts, and skills to awaken thought and present challenge.

Consequently, mathematics has an influence on the primary school curriculum; an influence that has not been realized in the past. Neither has it been appreciated that changes in the primary school curriculum have accompanied changes in the teaching of mathematics. Language development is extremely important. It is children's means of interpreting and communicating their thought to others, and its importance should not be minimized, but the function and significance of mathematics in the curriculum must be recognized also. The attitude to mathematics teaching in primary schools needs reappraisal. The subject should not be treated as a component which the primary school teacher has to teach. It should be approached with concern and a realization of how it influences the curriculum to expand the landscape.

Knowledge is a whole, and mathematics a part of this whole. Mathematics is a cultural subject, has practical uses, is a basic language, and encourages ordered and logical thought. These values should be realized and catered for in the primary school curriculum as children refer to them constantly in school activities. Validity exists for a mathematics policy across the curriculum.

Some educationalists will refute this as an over-emphasis of mathematics in the curriculum, but it pinpoints present shortcomings in the primary school. There is a need to define the purpose of the curriculum, and specify what is meant and what is intended with assumptions that evolve teaching strategies for children to develop as individuals who can think. Although learning is a continuous process and children vary in learning capability, a teacher's task is to provide a learning climate through stimulation and opportunities that will motivate children to learn. An active, inquiring, challenging, understanding, mathematically inspired primary education depends upon association based on reciprocal personal relationships, and is the means whereby children's landscapes expand. Unless the primary school curriculum is interpreted in this way, Jane and her contemporaries will remain in a barren wilderness instead of exploring an enchanted forest that has ever-increasing beauty. Perhaps, then, more children will say, 'Oh, good, I'll like that'.

REFERENCE

ROWLANDS, C. (1979, 17 September). 'Maths Teachers Must Try Harder', *Daily Mail*.

Index

83, 90, 93, 96, 109-10
Planning, 23, 24, 91
Theory, 14, 21

Danzig, T., 39
Dearden, R.F., 86, 89
De'Ath, S., 43, 67
Department of Education and Science, 50
Development, 10, 29, 38, 78
  Cognitive, 61, 63, 109
  Language, 21, 31, 41, 42, 125
  Level of, 24, 46, 59, 61, 62, 75, 93, 96, 100, 110, 117
  Mathematical, 41, 58, 71, 74-5, 88
  Pyschological, 31, 62-3, 70-1, 90, 92, 110
  of Vocabulary, 41, 64
Dewey, John, 16, 19
Downey, M., 66

Education Act, 1870, 16
Education Act, 1944, 17, 50, 73
Education Officers, 78
Environment, 17, 22, 37-8, 41, 52, 61, 63, 67, 89, 94-5, 99
Essex test, 18, 100, 107
Evaluation, 21, 67, 78, 109-20
Evetts, J., 70
Examinations, 116-117
  Eleven-plus, 18, 19, 20, 73, 74, 99, 116.
Experience:
  and Abstract thought, 91
  and Concrete thought, 91
  Learning, 21, 58, 80, 109
  Logico-mathematical, 38-41, 45, 90, 94
  Physical, 38, 41, 45

Feedback, 115-16
Fleming, C.M., 16
Formal classes, 101-4, 120
Froebel, Friedrich Wilhelm (1782-1852), 16
Froome, S., 66, 102

Gagne, R.M., 42
Gardner, K.L., 86-9
Glenn, J.A., 70, 71, 86-9
Global comparison, 27
Goddard, N., 51
Good, R.L., 68
Goodacre, E.J., 67
Green, A., 55, 57, 65

Ability, 21-2, 39-40, 66, 73, 90
  Mixed, 31, 74, 78, 79, 81, 83, 86, 90, 92, 95, 96, 115
Arithmetic, 16, 17, 30, 70, 71, 122, 123
Assessment, 67-8, 109, 112, 114-20
Association of British Chambers of Commerce, 122

Backhouse, J.K., 39, 40
Bantock, G.H., 102
Barron, J., 103
Behaviour see Pupil behaviour
Bennett, N., 102, 104
Black Papers, 101
Bloom, B.S., 21
Blyth, W.A.L., 51
Booth, T., 67
Brophy, J.E., 68
Bruner, J.S., 32, 39
Bullock Report (1975), 9, 84, 85, 86
Burns, P.C., 43
Burt, Sir Cyril Lodowic, 16
Byers, V., 39, 40, 41, 43, 44

Chain learning, 42
Changes in primary education, 73, 78, 101
Child, D., 118
Choat, E., 22, 23, 30, 43, 48, 67, 80, 88, 95, 98
Clarke, N., 104, 105-7
Comprehensive education, 18-19, 74, 101
Conceptualization, 22, 37, 39-41, 42, 45, 54, 59, 88, 91, 113, 119
Crawford, G.W.J., 101
Curriculum, 8-10, 12, 14, 19, 20
  Aims of, 20, 21, 67
  Content, 21, 23, 31, 58, 59, 67, 70, 71, 79, 89, 111
  Design of, 9, 15, 16, 19, 29, 98, 99
  Evaluation, 21, 67, 78, 109-20
  Integration, 84-5, 86, 89, 91
  Knowledge, 21, 22, 23
  Mathematics policy, 86, 90
  Objectives, 21, 23, 34, 52, 67, 69, 78,

Gribble, J., 21
Grouping, 74, 93, 94, 111
    see also Vertical grouping

Hadow Report, 1931, 16, 17,1 73
Hancox, D., 29-30
Headteacher, power of, 53, 78, 118
Hennessy, V., 11
Her Majesty's Inspectors, 78
Herscovics, N., 39, 40, 41, 43, 44
Hirst, P.H., 23, 59, 60, 61, 62
Home influence, 55-6, 60, 67, 95

ILEA Mathematics Inspectorate, 107,
    116, 119
Individualism, 14, 22-3, 31, 54, 63, 74,
    78, 79, 83, 90, 94, 96, 100, 111-12
Industrialization and education, 16
Informal classes, 101-4, 120
Institute of Mathematics, 104, 105, 107
Integration of curriculum content,
    84-5, 86, 89, 91
    and Mathematics, 86-92
Integrated day, 79-81, 96, 111
Intellectual capacity, 33, 90, 92, 110
    Child differences, 16-17, 24, 57
Interest, children's, 67, 70, 71, 81-3, 93
    Psychological, 62-3, 70-1
Intuition, 39-40, 45, 89

Jacobson, L., 67, 68
Jane, 26-7, 37, 47-9, 123-4
Judgement, 22

Kerr, J.F., 21, 109
Kline, M., 28
Kohl, H., 89
Krathwohl, D.R., 21

Language:
    Development, 21, 31, 41, 42, 125
    Structure, 41
Lazenby, M., 23
Learning:
    Principles of, 92-4, 109
    Psychology of, 70-1, 110
    Structured, 102
Levy, A., 30
Lippitt, R., 93
Logic, 15, 20, 38
    and Mathematics, 15, 20-1, 23, 38,
    40, 70
Logical thinking, 38-9, 92, 125

MacDonald, B., 109

McIntyre, D., 67-8
McPhillimy, W.N., 43, 44
Maslow, A.H., 61, 62
Mathematics:
    Abstract, 17, 88
    Basic processes, 10, 12, 15, 49, 53, 57,
    99
    Concepts, 88, 100,*see also*
    Conceptualization and Integration,
    87-92
    Language of, 15, 100, 125
    Logical approach, 15, 20-1, 23, 28,
    38, 70, 71, 86, 92, 94, 100, 125
    Primary, 7, 14-24, 53, 100, 125
    Role of, 10, 28, 96, 100
    and Symbols, 40-1, 48, 91
    Understanding, 36-46, *see also*
    Understanding
    Use of in the environment, 17, 22,
    37-8, 41, 52, 56, 61, 63, 67, 89, 94-5,
    99
Mathematics, learning of, 27-35, 37, 96
    Concept acquisition, 37, 39-42, 45, 94
Mathematics, teaching of, 8, 19, 32-5,
    52-3, 110
    Aim of, 34-5, 55, 57
    Cooperative, 76-9
    and Curriculum design, 9, 15, 16, 19,
    29, 98, 99
    Disagreements on, 26-35
    Organization, 64-5, 67, 76, 79-80, 92,
    111-15
    Role-expectation, 52-3, 65, 67, 68,
    91, 93, 110
    Role-set, 51-3, 55, 65
    Structured organization, 30, 52, 92
    Team, 8, 19, 31, 75-6, 77-9
    Techniques, 14, 46
    Vertical grouping, 8, 31, 76-9, 93
Matthews, J., 88
Meaningful learning, 43-5
Montessori, Maria (1870-1952), 16
Morrell, D., 60, 61
Morrison, A., 67-8
Moseley, D., 67
Motivation in learning, 23, 24, 32, 57,
    58, 61, 62, 67, 91, 92, 110

Nash, R., 68
Needs, children's, 61-3, 65, 67, 70, 93,
    96
Nuffield 'Checking Up' Guides, 119
Nuffield Mathematics Project, 54
Nursery schools and mathematics, 8,
    124

Objectives in teaching, 34, 52, 67, 78,
    90, 93, 109-10
  Elements of, 23, 31
  in Opposition, 29
  Psychological, 21, 23, 29, 31, 62-3,
    70-1, 90, 92, 110
  see also Curriculum, objectives
Open plan schools, 75, 78, 79, 101
Organization, 59, 64-5, 67, 76, 79-80,
    92, 111-115.

Palmer, R., 80
Perception, 38
Peters, R.S., 59, 60, 61, 62
Piaget, J., 7, 19, 38, 102, 119
Pidgeon, D., 109
Pinn, D.M., 101
Play, learning through, 11-12, 94, 113
Plowden Report (1967), 85
Progressives, 98
Project selection, 82-5, 95
  Mathematical approach, 87-9
Pyschological factors, 21, 23, 29, 31,
    62-3, 70-1, 90, 92, 110
Pupil achievement expectations, 68-9,
    108-20
Pupil assessment, 67-8, 109, 112, 114-20
Pupil behaviour, 66, 77, 80

Rae, G., 80
Records, 115
Renton, A.I.G., 86-9
Richmond, W.K., 23
Riedesel, C.A., 43
Robertson, J., 67
Rogers, V.R., 103
Rosenthal, R., 67, 68
Rote learning, 16, 17, 20, 21, 28, 30, 33,
    37, 40, 43, 44, 45, 99, 119
  Meaningful, 43-5
Rowlands, C., 122
Rs (the three), retention of, 26, 101, 104

Sharp, R., 55, 57, 65
Sime, M., 88
Skemp, R.R., 33, 36, 37, 39, 45
Skills, 35, 37, 53, 59, 92, 96, 114
  Analysis, 21-3
  Basic, 98-100, 104, 120
  Mathematical, 70, 88
  Synthesis, 21-3
Smith, Leslie A., 7, 90
Socialization, 51, 55, 56, 69, 70
Society and education, 16, 50-1, 63,
    108, 120
Sociological impact, 21, 103, 104

Specialization, 82-4, 86, 90, 91, 111
Standards of education, 9, 78, 98-101,
    108, 122, 124
Stenhouse, L., 98
Streaming, 17, 18, 19, 73-4, 78, 93, 115
Sumner, R., 105, 107
Symbols, 40-1, 48, 91

Tables, mathematical, 11, 30, 58, 95,
    117, 123
  'Recitation' of, for and against, 29-30
TAMS test, 100
Teaching climate, 93
Teaching programme:
  Discovery methods, 102
  Methods, 59, 67, 74-96, 113-20, 122
  Psychological approach, 21, 29, 30,
    33, 90
Teachers:
  Characteristics, 68-9
  Participation in play, 11-12, 94, 113
  Personal relationship with pupils, 24,
    59-60, 61, 63, 111, 125
  Providing stimulation, 24, 57, 58, 63,
    66, 91, 92, 125
  Qualifications, 32, 101
  Responsibilities, 9, 24, 50-71
  Role of, 51, 57
  Training, 102
Tests, 105-8, 117-19
  Conservation ('concept'7, 119-20
  Diagnostic, 118-19
  Standardized, 118
Textbooks, 8, 16, 52, 93-5, 112, 113
Thouless, R.H., 92
Troutman, A.P. 58

Understanding, learning with, 10, 28,
    30-1, 33, 36-46, 70, 103
  Formal, 39-42, 44
  Instrumental, 33, 36-7, 39, 40, 42, 44,
    45, 71, 90, 103, 104, 113
  Intuitive, 39-40, 45
  Relational, 33, 34, 36-7, 39-46, 71,
    103, 104, 113

Vertical grouping, 8, 31, 76-9, 93

Wall, W.D., 59
Ward, M., 53, 54, 55, 105-7
Watson, F.R., 86, 89
Wheatley, D., 18, 100
White, R.K., 93
Whitehead, A.N., 20
Wiseman, S., 109
Wood, H.B., 22-3